Paris Postcards

THE GOLDEN AGE

Library of Congress Cataloging-in-Publication Data
Pitt, Leonard, 1941-
Paris postcards : the golden age / by Leonard Pitt
p. cm.
Includes bibliographical references.
ISBN 978-1-58243-526-8

1. Paris (France)—History—1870-1940—Pictorial works.
2. Paris (France)—Social life and customs—Pictorial works. 3. Postcards—France—Paris—History.
4. Americans—France—Paris—History—20th century. I. Title.
DC707.P542 2010
944'.361081—dc22
2009024440

Cover and interior design by Alvaro Villanueva
Printed in Canada

COUNTERPOINT
2117 Fourth Street
Suite D
Berkeley, CA 94710

www.counterpointpress.com

Distributed by Publishers Group West

10 9 8 7 6 5 4 3 2 1

Paris Postcards
THE GOLDEN AGE

by

Leonard Pitt

COUNTERPOINT
BERKELEY

To my brothers, my son, and to the memory of my parents.

Acknowledgements

Many people have helped in the making of this book. Among them, Donald Galfond, Pamela Prince, Mark Liebman, Christian Deflandre of the *Musée de la Carte Postale* in Antibes, France, Jean Verot of the French postcard club—*the Cercle français des collectioneurs des cartes postales,* and the staff of the *Musée de la Poste* in Paris.

Contents

Introduction

❦

When I lived in Paris in the 1960s booksellers along the Seine sold old postcards of the city literally by the millions for ten centimes apiece. That's one U.S. penny. The French were not particularly interested in views of their city then, and nor was I. I bought a few cards and brought them back with me to Berkeley, California where I settled in 1970. Now far from Paris, I began looking at my small collection nostalgically and wished that I had bought more.

Then one day while strolling through a local flea market I came across a stack of Paris postcards from around 1900. "What a coincidence," I thought. Here were charming views of all the boulevards and monuments I knew so well, souvenirs bought by Americans doing the European Grand Tour to be mailed back home. I bought them all.

About a week later I happened into an antique store and came upon another stack of Paris postcards circa 1900. I snapped them up. A few days later, another visit to an antique store and bingo, another handful. By now I was hooked. The beauty of the cards, the amount of detail packed into something so small was compelling. Under a magnifying glass you could see individual expressions and relationships between people missed by the casual glance. By now a goner, I began making the rounds every weekend to flea markets and antique stores in hunt of more cards, and I was not disappointed.

I didn't get back to Paris until 1975. With visions of postcards filling my mind I rushed down to the bookstalls on the Seine expecting to buy handfuls at bargain prices. Oops, too late! Postcards had become big business in France and their cost had skyrocketed. The French and I were in perfect synch: we had both grown nostalgic for Paris at the same time. Cards that were barely a quarter a piece at home now cost dollars in Paris. Still, my collection grew.

Somewhere in the late 1970s, the postcards began drying up in California. Visits to the same haunts turned up fewer and fewer cards until there simply weren't any more. Then it dawned on me what was happening. Traveling to Europe was the grand vogue around 1900 and Paris was on every itinerary. Wealthy Americans from the San Francisco Bay Area were sailing to Europe in droves. By the 1970s these once-happy travelers had already departed for the celestial Champs Elysées. The postcards these travelers had collected, certainly a cherished part of the family estate, must have been left with a younger generation who, not feeling the same attachment, were suddenly putting them on the market. I just happened to be at the right place at the right time.

While my nostalgia for Paris was clear, what accounts for the French nostalgia for Paris?

In the late 1960s and early 1970s, an aggressive modernism began changing the face of the city with urban projects of a scale and design that were a radical break from the past. On the Left Bank the fifty-six-story Maine Montparnasse skyscraper shot up like a fire-spitting behemoth declaring that a new, more modern day had come. The demolition and reconstruction of Les Halles, the central markets on the Right Bank—for centuries the belly of Paris, in the words of Emile Zola—drove the point home more so. The future is here and you'd better get used to it!

To the west of Paris, La Defense was going up at breakneck speed, implanting a mini-Manhattan within Métro reach of the city center and obscuring a pristine view through the Arc de Triomphe that Parisians had enjoyed since the the early 1800s.

The French didn't have to leave Paris to grow nostalgic. Paris had left them. The resurgence of the postcard was understandable. Parisians were looking over their shoulders watching the city they knew sail off into the sunset, and postcards were a link with that past.

One day, a friend casually remarked that the colored postcards had been tinted by hand. I was taken aback. Thoroughly modern me, I assumed the cards were printed in color. Hand tinted! In our high-tech age where reproduction of the highest quality can be done at home with no skill at all, the cards suddenly took on the luster of little works of art. I began looking at them more closely, examining them in detail. Two cards that I thought were identical turned out to be the same photograph but tinted with different colors. Maybe someone had varied the tinting for their own amusement, or they were tinted by different people?

A couple of years ago I began organizing my postcards, scanning and putting them into albums sorted by arrondisements. Seeing them organized in this way was like seeing them for the first time. Two things struck me. First, the photographs show us a Paris that has long since disappeared. The city has none of today's garishness. There is a rhythm and way of life many of us long for and try to recreate in our own lives. Streets are unencumbered by automobiles. People stand leisurely in the middle in casual conversation. The fashions of the day were not nearly as comfortable or practical as today's, but oh, what allure!

Secondly, the messages people wrote to family and loved ones back home! Charm is not wanting here. It's all so evocative of the American experience of Paris at the early part of the 20th century when Paris was a place very far away.

THE BIRTH OF THE POSTCARD

Few people would believe that something as common as the postcard could have such a dramatic history. In the 1870s, before electricity and telephones were part of every household, the introduction of the postcard revolutionized communication and created the first form of social networking equivalent to today's e-mail.

Many deplored the novelty, certain that this new type of message, shorter than the traditional letter, meant that people would forget how to write. Similar objections surfaced when the first photographs began appearing on postcards in the 1890s. It was feared that people, awash in images, would forget how to read. For the educated classes, postcards were considered vulgar. Abbreviations were crude, no better than slang. A missive without proper introductions and salutations was objectionable.

But the public knew better. By the 1870s the number of postcards going through the mail was staggering. In 1875 thirty-seven million postcards were purchased in Germany. In 1876, in England, the number was seventy-nine million. In Austria that same year twenty million postcards went through the mail. Whole industries grew up around postcard production and became key to national economies, employing tens of thousands of people.

By the time the postcard reached its Golden Age, from around 1895 to 1915, collecting became a phenomenon and no home was complete without a postcard album or two in the parlor, second in importance only to the bible. Many hours were spent perusing, comparing, sorting, discussing, and showing postcards to friends and family. People traveling anywhere made solemn promises to mail postcards back home to friends and loved ones to add to their collections. Every city and town had legions of postcard sellers, postcard hawkers, postcard racks, and whole shops that sold nothing but postcards. Conversations were full of talk about postcards: who was selling what, what views were favorites, etc. By 1900, there were international postcard shows, local postcard clubs, and magazines devoted to postcards.

The invention of the first "official" postcard goes to John P. Charlton of Philadelphia, Pennsylvania in 1861—official because he actually patented his idea and established commercial production of the postcard. Unfortunately nothing is known about Charlton or his enterprise or what led him to conceive the idea. We do know that he didn't keep the patent long and within a year had sold it to H.L. Lipman, who produced cards that were sold to businesses who in turn printed their message on the card for advertising purposes. Only four of these cards are known to exist.

Lipman's enterprise ended in 1873 when the U.S. government, in the best tradition of free enterprise, began production of its own pre-stamped postcards, thus imposing a monopoly on a budding industry. Lipman was out of business. Sixty million of these government issued cards were sold in the first three months alone. It took an act of Congress to open the field once again to private publishers and printers with the Private Mailing Card Act of 1898.

Was there a link between the American and the European postcard? Was an American postcard mailed to Europe and, like a plant spore carried by the wind, did it sprout in a new land? No evidence supports this notion. It seems that the postcard was simply an idea whose time had come. And of all the countries in Europe, where did the idea germinate first and who was responsible?

To find out, we must travel to the small town of Stolp in the Kingdom of Prussia. In 1848, a gentleman walked into the local post office to inquire about the rate for a letter he wanted to send to Naples. The postal employee, seventeen-year-old Heinrich von Stephan, told him it would take a few minutes to make the calculation. Neither Germany or Italy existed yet. In their place were a number of small independent states each with their own postal rates based on weight and distance.

To arrive at the correct rate of postage, von Stephan had to figure the distance the letter would travel through each state, e.g., Thurn and Taxis, Lombardy, Venice, Tuscany, etc. Imagine the conscientious young man poring over heavy volumes with onion skin-thin pages as he made his calculation. Patience was the order of the day.

The exasperated gentleman implored von Stephan to find a better method in the future. "I'll do my best," he replied. And he did. Von Stephan eventually became Postmaster General of a unified Germany and was one of the founders of the 1874 Universal Postal Union, an international organization that standardized postal rates throughout Europe. He was held in the highest esteem not only by his own countrymen but around the world. His portrait has adorned the stamps of countries such as Switzerland, Namibia, Chile, Nicaragua, Gabon, and Botswana.

Constantly seeking ways to make the postal system more efficient, von Stephan attended the Austro-German postal conference held in Karlsruhe in 1865, where he presented a revolutionary idea based on a simple yet profound observation. The history of the letter, he explained, from the wax tablets of antiquity to the rolled form of the Middle Ages to the letter of his own day, was an evolution towards ever greater simplicity. But even "the present form of the letter" he said, was not simple enough. "Note paper must be selected and folded." The envelope must be "obtained and closed" and the "stamps affixed."

To complicate things further "convention necessitates something more than the bare communication." Von Stephan found this "irksome both to the sender and the receiver."

His idea was a "post-sheet" (*postblatt*), a piece of stiff paper the size of an envelope with the address on one side and a written message on the other. The card would be sold with the stamp printed on the card and would be mailed without an envelope. The postage would be as low as possible. Von Stephan was certain that his new *postblatt* would be useful for many occasions. People traveling, he said, could drop a simple note to tell loved ones of their safe arrival or ask for something they had forgotten. Not only was it well suited for "social purposes" but it could be used equally well for business transactions. The idea was given the fullest consideration but came up against stiff obstacles. For one, the proposed lower postal rate, it was argued, would reduce revenue. And there was the insurmountable problem of establishing a standard rate between the different states of the German Confederation. Von Stephan's idea was rejected.

It took four years for the idea to surface again, this time in Vienna, Austria. In 1869 Dr. Emmanuel Hermann, professor of political economy, submitted an article to the local newspaper, the *Neue Frie Presse* (*New Free Press*), in which he presented observations, not unlike those of von Stephan, that a majority of correspondence was of such a simple nature that the trouble of writing the letter almost outweighed the content of the letter. Hermann suggested a simple card, uncovered, with a stamp affixed at a rate lower than a standard letter. The benefit would be two-fold, he explained: The public would enjoy a cheaper rate of postage and the government would see an increase in mail.

Because Austria was a sovereign nation unto itself with a unified postal system—unlike Prussia which was a tangle of postal administrations—the idea of the postcard found favor with the Austrian Postmaster General. On September 22, 1869 an official decree announced the creation of Europe's first mass-produced postcard.

Originally known as *Correspondenz-Kart*, this idea, so obvious to us today, needed an assortment of rules and regulations to inform both the public and postal employees as to how to use this new means of communication.

"They are to be mailed openly, without any seal whatsoever . . . they will be used for short communication to all places of the Austro-Hungarian Monarchy regardless of distance." For anyone not sure how to proceed "The address has to appear on the front side of the card . . . the back of the card is to be used for the written message." One could write in ink, pencil, or even a colored pencil. But above all, "care should be taken that the writing is legible."

The new postcard was issued on October 1, 1869 and success was immediate. Even though the new card was only allowed to be mailed within the borders of the Austro-Hungarian Monarchy, in the first three months 2,926,102 were sold. It didn't take long for the German states to see that they had missed out, and on July 1, 1870, the North German Confederation issued its postcard. On the first day of issue in Berlin alone 45,468 were sold.

The next three years saw other European countries follow suit. In 1870, Belgium, Luxembourg, Great Britain, and Switzerland. In 1871, Holland, Denmark, Sweden and Norway. In 1872, Russia. And in 1873, Serbia, Romania and Spain. Notice that France is missing.

THE POSTCARD IN FRANCE

France's entry into the world of the postcard was fraught with difficulty. First of all there was the Franco-Prussian war. Barely two weeks after the first postcard had been issued in the German States, France declared war on Prussia. Postal matters were not high on anyone's list of concerns. Even though by 1873 the postcard had not been adopted in France, it was known to the French postal administration and in fact had been used during the Prussian siege of Paris between September 21, 1870, and January 28, 1871, when quantities of cards were carried beyond siege lines by hot-air balloon. Once the war was over, France continued to hemorrhage through a Civil War, the infamous Commune, that only ended with La Semaine Sanglante (the Bloody Week), May 21ST to May 28TH, when as many as twenty thousand Parisians died at the hands of government forces in fierce acts of reprisal. Much of the city had been destroyed in the fighting. The postal system—what was left of it—could hardly think about postcards. They had disappeared from use.

By June the hostilities were over and the nation began pulling itself back together. In August the French Parliament convened to discuss how to rebuild the decimated postal system. With the administration facing a huge deficit the solution for many was easy: raise postal rates. Enter Louis Wolowski. If ever there was a hero for the French postcard, this was the man.

Wolowski immigrated to France from Poland in 1831 and became a naturalized citizen. Early on he distinguished himself by receiving a chair at the Conservatoire des Arts et Metiers and later being made a member of the National Assembly. Most notably he created one of France's most important financial institutions, the Credit Foncier, which was responsible for much of the money behind Haussmann's public works, which transformed Paris in the 1850s and '60s.

On August 23, 1871, Wolowski took the floor of the National Assembly. Rather than raising rates, he argued, that the solution was to lower them. Increase the social interactions between people, and the number of letters going through the mail will grow. The public wealth, he said, can be measured in relation to the growth in correspondence between people, and this can only be achieved by lowering rates. Those who pushed for higher rates argued that the gain could amount to as much as twenty-two million francs. Wolowski countered. "While other countries advance, we're going to slide backwards, and all this for a hypothetical increase in revenue." "Sometimes," he added, "in financial matters, one and one do not make two." While some agreed, the majority voted against. His proposal was defeated. Rates went up.

Not to be discouraged, Wolowski continued with an even more radical idea: "An innovation that has been accepted almost everywhere in continental Europe"—the "carte postale," mailed without envelope and posted at half the cost of a letter. On one side, the address, the other, a message. "Show us one!" someone called out. Wolowski pulled out a postcard and held it up for all to see. One can imagine these bearded and goateed gentlemen in their three piece suits leaning forward as they squinted over eye glasses perched on noses to examine this oddity from a distance.

Wolowski went on to defend his idea:

"Here is an example of a correspondence card that has been used by the English since last October. Do you know the results! More than fifty-eight million were sold in the first trimester. For the year the number has surpassed 100 million."

He concluded his argument with examples from England, the United States and Germany showing that after the postcard had been introduced the number of letters posted had actually increased.

Wolowski then proposed an amendment to the current postal laws with a description of the postcard and what purpose it was to serve. A vote was taken and his article was declared "adopted."

But not so fast.

Those against the idea protested that the vote was not fair, that the idea had not been presented in a clear and concise enough fashion, and that some deputies voted not understanding the real content of the proposal. The vote was taken again. This time Wolowski lost. A friend suggested that his proposal might do bet-

ter if it was part of a larger proposal for postal reform, and for that he would have to wait.

And wait he did, for over a year and a half. In December 1872 Wolowski stood before the National Assembly and introduced his idea again:

"When I had the honor of making a similar proposal sixteen months ago, I was told that the results were not yet in, that I had to wait. Well, experience has shown us the value of this idea again and again, not only in England and Germany but in many other European countries. Today there are only two countries in Europe that have the distinction of being not only without the postcard, but without there even being any discussion of it. Those two countries are France and Turkey."

To drive home his point, he offered the observation that before the introduction of the postcard in England, the number of letters increased 4% per year. After the postcard, this figure had risen to 6% per year.

Wolowski met resistance again. A

member of this august body, a Mr. Cail-
leux from the Sarthe region, was adamant
about not wanting to launch the postal
administration into a financial adven-
ture, and haggled over numbers and the
fear of losing revenue. He insisted that if
the idea was to go forward it had to be
tested first on a small scale.

But Wolowski had an important ally,
Mr. Germain Rampont-Léchin, a deputy
from the Yonne region who also happened
to be the Postmaster General of France.
His short term of only two years, from
1871 to 1873, was well timed for Wolowski. While he admitted that he did not sup-
port Wolowski's idea the first time around,
this time he was firmly behind him. Some
have suggested that part of the resistance
on the part of deputies had to do with the
war still fresh in everyone's mind. They
did not want to adopt an idea, no matter how good, that had been successful
in Germanic countries first. Discussion
ensued, arguments flared. The amendment was put to a vote and success! The
date was December 19, 1872. On the eve

of the postcard's introduction in France,
Wolowski wrote a seven-page article laying out the virtues of the postcard. It is
worth the read—see the appendix.

The postcard was to go on sale in
France on January 1, 1873. News of its
imminent release was met with such enthusiasm by the public that the government
had to issue a notice stating that because
of "the impossibility of obtaining a suf-
ficient number to meet consumer demand,
the sale of postcards has been postponed
until the 15TH." National printing presses
were so overwhelmed that private printers were called into action. It didn't take
long for all doubt about the postcard
to evaporate in government circles. The
number sold in the first week in France
was an astonishing 7,412,700.

PROTESTS AGAINST
THE POSTCARD

Despite this impressive figure, many
people still objected to the postcard. One
reason was the lack of discretion. Written

correspondence was highly personal with
an aura of secrecy around it. Receiving a
letter was an event noticed by everyone
in a household and its opening often had
its own family ritual. Before the envelope was commonplace many letters were
cleverly folded so that the letter made its
own envelope. Often a letter was not even
referred to as a letter, but rather as a *pli*,
a fold. To see one of these early letters
folded so cleverly is to look upon a marvel
of ingenuity and careful attention.

Sealing a letter with wax had its own
ritual too, and a man easily distinguished
himself by his manner of sealing his letter. Men used bold, red wax. Women,
more feminine pastel colors. Because of
this, seals were enough to identify the
sex of the sender. Postcards were con-
fusing. Without seeing the name of the
sender one had no idea who had written.
To solve this problem the US government
issued larger postcards for men, smaller
for women. This solution was not popular
and was withdrawn after a short time.

For many the uncovered message was

disconcerting, a breach of modesty. Anyone could read it: the mailman, the doorman, the concierge, other people in house. This type of exposure was unfamiliar in the buttoned-down 19TH century. Writing something personal for all to see on a postcard was tantamount to walking down the street naked.

Some postal workers could not resist the temptation to sneak a peek at the messages and this caused an uproar. The postal administration, aware of the problem, sent out notices to all employees citing abuses of this sort and emphasized that even though the postcard traveled at a cheaper rate than a letter, it was imperative that it benefit from the same confidentiality as a letter.

One famous case took place in Normandy barely a month after the postcard had been introduced in France. A young girl working in the post office of a small town read a somewhat compromising postcard sent by the local parish priest to a woman in his congregation. The girl not only read the message aloud to her colleagues but copied it. Scandal ensued. The priest brought a lawsuit against the girl on the basis that she had violated a secret. The judge found the girl not guilty on the basis that an open missive could not be considered a secret. The priest appealed and won. The girl was convicted.

Defamation was another issue. It is hard to believe today, but some people actually used the postcard to defame or slander others and this led to lawsuits. In many countries important questions arose forcing a reconsideration of the very nature of libel. To write a letter carrying an accusation is not libelous because, being closed, it is private. Make the accusation public and you have libel. The postcard was somewhere in between. Because people for whom the card was not intended could read it, did this make it public? An Irish court said yes, citing the logic that "confidential communications must not be shouted across the street for all passers-by to hear." A court in Pennsylvania found otherwise, while a North Carolina court deemed that libel had occurred via postcard. Canada too looked at this issue in 1897 when a man sent a postcard to a doctor accusing him of being a "fakir" and "amateur doctor" and was found guilty of libel. The state of Ohio, on the other hand, disagreed. "It would not do to assume that because a postal card has been placed in the post office it has been read."

Concern was so great in Austria that state-issued postcards carried a disclaimer "The postal administration is not responsible for the contents of this communication."

Problems of confidentiality plagued the French postcard to the end of the century, and in 1899, the postal administration was obliged to send out yet another notice: "Employees are forbidden to 1. read postcards, 2. to send, forward or deliver any postcard bearing written insults or abusive expressions." These two directives seem mutually exclusive. How could one detect abusive messages without reading the card?

Clearly, for many, the postcard represented a cultural divide. The letter was of a slower, more genteel world. A world of consideration and politeness. The postcard was fast, curt, and abandoned all social formality. Many stationers looked down upon them and refused to carry them. Many photographers, used to producing yearly family portraits printed on quality paper and placed in expensive frames, felt compelled to print their photos on cheaper postcards and only did so begrudgingly. Many did not bend to the new fashion, certain that it was beneath them.

There is a parallel here with computers, cell phones and text messaging today. Some embrace the newness. Others come to it slowly, only after much hesitation, while others never take to it at all. If a letter is a horseless carriage, the postcard is a train moving at lightning speed. In 1901, *American Magazine* sounded the clarion call with an article, "Upon the Threatened Extinction of the Art of Letter Writing." An 1890 English manual of etiquette looked down on the postcard. "Don't conduct correspondence on postcards. It is questionable whether a note on a postcard is entitled to the courtesy of a response." In *A Guide to Reading For Young and Old*, a decline in "the art of letter writing" was blamed on the "unpardonable post card."

The younger generation had little trouble connecting with the postcard. In 1903, a young girl in Norway wrote about "a friend who is so foolish that he writes letters. Did you ever hear about anything so ridiculous? As if I care for a good-for-nothing letter. I cannot put a letter into my album, can I?"

A note written in 1900 by a British tourist parallels observations made today about the isolation of the laptop computer:

"You enter the railway station and everybody on the platform has a pencil in one hand and a postcard in the other. In the train it is the same thing. Your fellow travelers never speak. They have little piles of picture postcards on the seat beside them, and they write monotonously."

THE RISE, FALL, AND RISE OF THE POSTCARD

Before the postcard could achieve the level of cultural phenomenon, a number of obstacles had to be overcome. First there was the tangle of postal agreements between countries. When the postcard was first introduced, postal treaties between nations were a labyrinth of rules and tariffs that hindered all movement. In 1874 France had sixteen different postal agreements. Germany had seventeen. A letter traveling through more than one country was subject to multiple charges that ran up its cost to exorbitant levels. When the railroad was invented it was imperative that trains of all countries use a standard gauge track in order to make inter-continental rail travel possible. A similar uniformity was needed with the world's postal systems.

In 1874, an international postal congress was held in Berne, Switzerland, organized by none other than Heinrich von Stephan, the young postal clerk of Stolp, Prussia mentioned above. A sign of the confusion to be unraveled were the over 1,000 postal rates in effect between the countries attending. This international congress was a watershed. Out of it came the landmark General Postal Union, known today as the Universal Postal Union, an international organization that set a single rate for letters and postcards, thus eliminating many of the obstacles that had plagued the public for years.

And there was the postcard itself. Too dull. Used mostly for banal messages (unless you were a priest in Normandy), there was nothing to spark the imagination, nothing to inspire the public to value the postcard as a thing in itself. The only embellishment was a decorative border around the edge on the address side. Without photos or illustrations the postcard was simply an expedient. Private printers in France had gotten around state monopolies for years by printing advertisements on the blank side, but this was not enough to launch it into the affections of the mass public. To achieve this, the postcard had to go beyond the utilitarian to find an emotional

connection with the sender. It had to become part of their experience, an avenue of expression for the sender.

The perfect place for this to happen was at the 1889 Paris World's Fair. The hit of the fair was the new Eiffel Tower. Standing taller than any structure in the world, the tower was the fair's star attraction, with the added thrill that one could ascend to the top for spectacular views of Paris that few mortals had ever seen.

Three months after the fair opened a postcard with a small illustration of the Eiffel Tower went on sale at the tower itself. So banal today, this card, designed by Leon-Charles Libonis and published by the newspaper *Le Figaro*, gave the postcard a new dimension. Even though the image of the Eiffel Tower was only a vignette on the card, this was enough. The thrill of taking in the view from on high was funneled directly into the card, giving it an immediacy that made it even more appealing. With a post office installed on the tower, one could mail it immediately with an Eiffel Tower post-

mark. Nearly 300,000 cards were sold. This simple drawing of the Eiffel Tower was an important step in galvanizing the public's enthusiasm for the illustrated postcard in France.

It wasn't long before the photograph found its way onto the postcard too. There is more than one claim to this novel idea. The most interesting, however, is that of Dominique Piazza of Marseille. The story goes that Piazza had a friend who moved to Argentina. Growing homesick, this friend requested that Piazza send him photos of Marseille. Photos in those days were heavy affairs mounted on rigid board that were expensive to mail. In 1891 Piazza had the novel idea of placing several vignette photos of Marseille on the message side of the postcard.

As the public's interest in the picture postcard grew, new cheaper techniques of photo reproduction helped provide impetus to a growing industry. By 1907, France was producing 300 million postcards a year. That's nearly one million a day. In 1907, the estimated number of postcards sold worldwide was seven billion and this did not include cards bought for private collections and never mailed. In 1903, England posted 613 million postcards. Germany, one billion, 162 million. The U.S., 770 million. The world was gripped with postcard mania.

Postcard manufacturing became key to the French economy, employing as many as 33,000 people during the peak years of the card's Golden Age. And this is not counting the thousands of others peripheral to actual postcard production who earned a living wage from the craze: photographers, artists, wholesalers, retailers; manufacturers of printing presses; producers of paper, paint, ink, and brushes; the factories that turned out postcard albums, and on and on. "Eliminate the postal card and you throw an entire industry into the deepest crisis," said the President of a French Stamp Association in 1901.

With the postcard craze in full swing no street, passage, or dead end in Paris escaped the photographer's camera. A grand democratization gave equal value to everything in sight. Not only every city, town and hamlet, not only Paris and throughout France, but the world, in fact, found its place onto the postcard, for this was a worldwide phenomenon. In 1907, a

Вапнярка.—Vapnjarka. № 3.

This card illustrates how the world had become gripped by the postcard craze, with even the most remote corners being photographed. How many people might be interested in a view of this dirt road in an obscure village in the Russian Ukraine? Perhaps myself. My mother was born in the house on the left. On the porch stands my great-grandmother.

London journalist described the fever:

"Nobody need fear that there is any spot on the earth which is not depicted on this wonderful oblong. The photographer has photographed everything between the poles. He has snapshotted the earth. No mountain and no wave has evaded his omnipresent lens . . . he has hunted down every landscape and seascape on the globe . . . every bird and every beast has been captured by the camera. It is impossible to find anything that has not been frayed to a frazzle by photographers."

As the craze grew postcard sellers popped up everywhere, and everyone became a postcard seller. Vendors strolled the boulevards with portable racks displaying postcards for sale to those sitting at sidewalk cafés. Entire stores became postcard emporiums with walls and counters covered with masses of them. Atlantic City had ten such stores. One observer wrote, "Wherever you may go, be it hundred of miles from Paris, to the desert, on a glacier, to the summit of the highest peak, to the most abandoned stream you won't find a morsel of bread or a cup of water to quench your thirst, but you'll surely find postcards." Another wrote, the postcard "paralyzes the reasoning faculties."

Of all the aspects of postcard production, perhaps the most fascinating is the hand coloring of the cards. We know that stencils were cut from thin sheets of either zinc, copper or waxed paper. A steady hand and a trained eye guided a surgeon's scalpel in this delicate maneouvre. One stencil per color, and each postcard was colored individually. The colorists were young women sitting at large tables with stacks of postcard sheets before them. Color was applied with gouache or ink using a variety of brushes. Stenciling, known in French circles as *pochoir*, is an age-old technique and was already part of the culture of 19TH century France with greeting cards, playing cards, engravings, etc. The tinting of postcards followed naturally.

The city of Nancy in northeastern France became a center of postcard production. One of the biggest publishers, Albert Bergeret, opened two printing presses in 1898 with a handful of employees. Two years later he had thirty presses and a staff of 150. Bergeret alone turned out 300,000 postcards a day. Jules Royer opened his print shop in Nancy in 1870, producing engravings, lithographs, wedding invitations, and birth announcements. In 1884, he turned to postcards and by 1904, he had 250 people working all facets of production. Another major publisher, Humblot and Simon, had thirty-seven presses running by 1904. In Paris, Levy Bros. and Neurdin opened a shop with great success.

One factor to encourage the postcard's growth was the excellent mail service of the time, by today's standards unimaginably efficient. Post offices in France were open from 8 AM to 8 PM Monday through Saturday and until 5 PM on Sundays and holidays. In 1889, in Paris, there were 8 mail pick-ups a day. By 1901 the number had risen to ten. Deliveries were just as impressive. In 1907, there were seven per day, including Saturday and Sunday. A letter mailed by 9:15 AM was delivered by 1:40 PM. Outside Paris, where pick-ups and deliveries were less frequent, anyone who put a postcard into the mail by morning was assured that it would arrive at its destination in time with the message, "Arriving on train tonight at 7 PM."

A sign of the postcard's growing popularity were the postcard clubs that began appearing in many countries. In 1900, a club in Nancy had 2,400 members. Out of these clubs came an array of journals, reviews and magazines, all serving to galvanize interest in the postcard. France had twenty-three such publications devoted to the postcard. This surge of interest lead to huge postcard exhibitions—the Mac World of its day. Publishers, printers, and vendors from all corners set up tables and booths showing off their latest designs numbering in the thousands. The first such European Postcard Salon was held in Leipzig in 1898. Venice followed in 1899. Then in 1900, Budapest and Warsaw.

Such great interest in the postcard

gave free reign to the imagination, and publishers tried every angle in hopes of capturing the public's fancy. City views, country views, views of nature—peaks, crashing ocean waves, sunsets—humorous themes, political themes, news events, accidents, movie stars, and romance were all categories to suit every taste, whim, and fancy. Some of the more imaginative postcards featured phonograph discs that could be played with a metal wire attached, acting as a needle.

Within a relatively short period of time, a whole world had grown up around the postcard. Tens of thousands of jobs had been created, livelihoods (indeed fortunes) had been built upon them, people's lives and relationships were wrapped up in the postcard. But beyond the industry of the postcard there was the psychological world of the postcard, and the amount of real estate it occupied in the imagination of whole populations—just as computers do today—is impressive.

How long did this Golden Age last? Not as long in America as in Europe. One

reason was the Payne-Aldrich Tariff Act of 1909, created to counter the popularity of the German postcard. Germany had a long history of producing art works with superior printing and lithography techniques. This, combined with cheaper German labor, led most American pub-

Man selling postcards in a café.

lishers to have their postcards designed in America but printed in Germany. In January 1909, three million postcards a day were entering America from Germany through the port of New York alone. In total, 90% of the postcards sold in America were imports. For many this was a cause of consternation. "There is no good reason why the postcards used in this country . . . should not be manufactured by American labor. Give American labor a square deal and they will show results superior to foreign goods in time. It is hopeless to attempt to compete with the foreign manufacturers . . . and unless a favorable tariff is established it will mean a steady decline of the postcard industry and ultimately its ruin."

The tariff did succeed in staunching the flow of German postcards but it also wreaked havoc with the American postcard industry as the law of unintended consequences played out. The American postcard never rose to the level of its German competitor, and in time, the public's interest waned. In 1914, a magazine for pharmacists noted that "The picture postcard vogue is dying out." That same year fifteen American postcard companies closed.

And there was the war. Whatever the Payne-Aldrich Act could not achieve was accomplished by World War I. The German postcard industry fell into a shambles. World tourism came to an end. Yet, the postcard in Europe hung on longer. For millions of soldiers, the postcard was a lifeline to home, an inexpensive and easy way to stay in touch with loved ones. Sentimental cards of "Missing you," propaganda cards with pictures of the Kaiser being booted in the behind, or patriotic cards spurring soldiers on in their service flourished. The risqué cards France had become known for sold in great numbers and adorned many corners of the wartime landscape.

By the war's end, new technology was eclipsing the postcard. People were far more inundated with images in newspapers, magazines and the cinema. Plus there was the telephone, the radio, and greater use of the telegraph. Costs of postcard production rose as well, and with that, quality declined.

The postcard continued after the war, but never at the level it had achieved during its peak. One important change was that people no longer bought them as collectibles. In earlier years, many postcards were bought with no intention of being mailed, and went straight into albums. Now postcards were used and thrown away. For this reason it is easier to find cards from the period before 1920 than afterwards.

This period of decline of the postcard lasted for the next forty or fifty years. In the parlance of today's hard core collectors, those were the years of "purgatory." It was as if the prized Russian Fabergé eggs, sought after, coveted and prized, had suddenly turned into nothing more than, well, eggs ready for an omelet. The luster was gone.

Then, in the 1960s, things turned around. The first modern day postcard salon was held in Paris in 1965, and the following year a French postcard club was established: *Cercle français des collectioneurs des cartes postales* and its quarterly publication *Le Cartophile*. But it wasn't until 1975 that the first international postcard show was held in Paris. That was the watershed event that put the humble postcard back into the realm of big collectibles, and with that, prices soared.

Today, one sees postcards on sale in Paris at all the same tourist spots but the handwriting is on the wall. In the 1960s, no one I knew in Paris owned a telephone. Getting one installed meant waiting a year. The French Minister of Communication, in fact, is remembered for his comment that the telephone was no more than a gimmick. With so few telephones in those days, an ingenious form of communication was the *pneumatique*. Under the streets of Paris are an intricate network of vacuum tubes laid down in the 1860s connecting all the post offices of the city. Still in use in the 1960s, one could purchase *un pneu* at any post office, write a message,

and off it went in a whoosh across the city to the post office nearest the destination. Once it arrived it was taken directly and delivered to the address. From start to finish took about two hours, a magnificent feat in those days.

Placing a phone call to the States back then was a major event. This required a trip to the post office to make an appointment with a telephone operator. On the return one waited to be called. "Mr Pitt! Cabin three please!" Postcards in those days, therefore, were an essential part of living away from home. In 1966, Frank Staff wrote in *The Picture Postcard & its Origins*, "Today the picture postcard is still the best and most favoured means of keeping in touch ... [it] can truthfully be said to have been one of the most useful creations of all times."

Oh, how the world has changed. Cell phones and email undoubtedly signal the decline of the postcard. And that is the way of the world. The introduction of the automobile wiped out the culture of travel

by horse: buggies, wagons, wheelwrights, saddles, saddle makers, blacksmiths, harnesses, the now fanciful clothes, the lore. All gone.

Technology is a master of seduction. For good or for bad, it is not for us to question but only to follow. And follow we do. All we can hope for as each new wave of technology washes over us is that it does not diminish or isolate us, that it does not reduce our experience and make us smaller, but rather that it encourages us to grow and makes our minds and hearts larger.

And in the meantime we can be grateful for these remnants of the past that have been saved from the detritus of history to enrich us once again. And who knows. When television first came onto the scene all the talk was about the demise of radio. That post-mortem certainly went on hold. So maybe one day the postcard will rise again. Or maybe it is time here for a quote from the Everly Brothers, "Dreeeeeam, dream, dream, dream!"

CARTE POSTALE

destinée à circuler à découvert en France et en Algérie,

dans l'intérieur d'une même ville

ou dans la circonscription du même bureau.

PRIX : **10** CENTIMES.

(Loi du 20 Décembre 1872.)

Rue Taitbout
Bud. 3

M *Gaudri cité desmartir* *16*

L'adresse seule doit être mise de ce côté de la carte.
L'autre côté est réservé à la correspondance.

Lorsque la carte est à destination
d'une ville, indiquer très-exactement la
rue et le numéro de la maison.

One of the first French postcards, 1872. Opposite side is blank. *Actual size.*

Beginnings

*T*his is the postcard (facing page) that revolution-ized communication in its day—a government issued postcard with one side for the address, and the other side for the message. So banal today, in the late 1870s this redrew the social landscape. Because no one had ever seen such a thing instructions were printed on the address side. The top reads, "Postcard meant to be mailed uncovered," meaning without an envelope. On the left edge, "Only the address should be written on this side of the card. The other side is reserved for the correspondence." On the right edge, "Write the number of the house clearly and legibly." The postage rate printed on the card, 10 centimes, indicated that this card could be mailed only within the city in which it was posted. Cards that traveled from city to city cost 15 centimes.

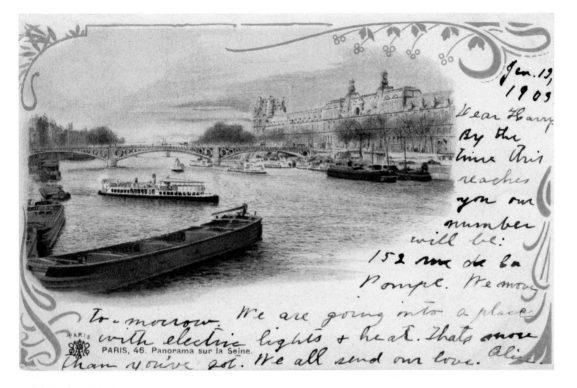

THE SEINE. When illustrations were introduced on postcards they had to compete for space with the message, as on this card. The other side was still reserved for the address only. The postcard as we know it today, the divided back, with a line down the middle separating the address from the message, was introduced in France in 1904—but not in the U.S. until 1907. The divided back was a boon to collectors, who often complained that the prized illustrations had been compromisd by the message.

January 13, 1903
Dear Harry,

By the time this reaches you our number will be 152 rue de la Pompe. We move tomorrow. We are going into a place with electric lights & heat. That's more than you've got. We all send our love.   —Alice

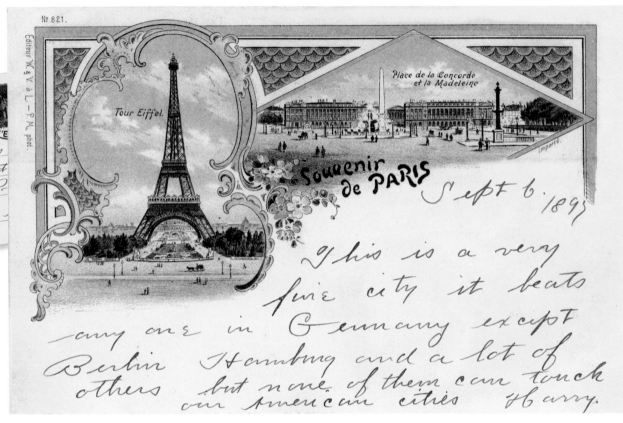

September 6, 1897
 This is a very fine city. It beats any one in Germany except Berlin, Hamburg and a lot of others. But none of them can touch our American cities.
        —Harry

On a tour in France | Paris France, 7/22/06
Have covered a | with the motor cycle
Expect to return | delightful 400 miles.
Havre & Ostende | to Belgium via
With sincer— | in a few days.
| est wishes to all.
| As ever,
| Bain

PARIS - Notre-Dame.

NOTRE-DAME. The "divided back" not long after its introduction in France in 1904. Notice that this American correspondent, Bain, was not yet used to this format and continued to write the address across the whole card with his message on the photo side. Clearly he was having a fine time in Europe. Note that the card is written in pencil. Before ballpoint pens, fountain pens were not always convenient, especially for someone on the road. This gentleman most certainly kept a pen knife in his pocket. Imagine the fun of cycling around France on a motorcycle in 1906. Where were the gas stations?

July 22, 1906
On a tour in France with the motorcycle. Have covered a delightful 400 miles. Expect to return to Belgium via Havre & Ostende in a few days. With sincerest wishes to all.
—As ever, Bain

CARTE POSTALE
Tous les pays étrangers n'acceptent pas la correspondance au recto
(Se renseigner à la poste.)

Correspondance | Adresse du destinataire

Miss Olive Yo—
593 Merrimac St.
Oakland
California
U. S. A.

My Dear Georgette,

I hope you have not this postal because I know you have so many of Paris. I am going to see Nancy next Wednesday. Mama and Papa are in Italy now. When they come back we are all going to Switzerland together.

—Love, Loulou

PONT AU CHANGE AND PALAIS DE JUSTICE.

Loulou has made progress over Bain. She has written the address in the right place but needlessly written across the photo, leaving the message space on the card empty. The message tells us that Georgette is a collector.

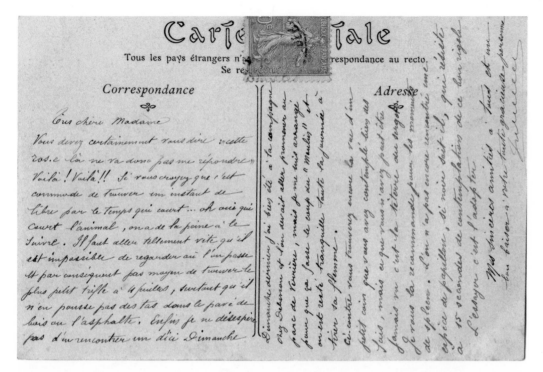

Hand written or printed? A Frenchman writes a letter from San Francisco in 1852.

THERE ONCE WAS A THING CALLED PENMANSHIP. *Actual size.* Writing with a steel tipped pen from an ink bottle lends itself to a certain style of writing not possible with a fountain pen, a pencil or a ballpoint pen. It was not unusual for people to write postcards of surprising length. The card above is a fine example, but does not compare to the man in Norway who was known for a postcard on which he wrote a message of 48,000 words.

A letter of 1857 with great style, folded upon itself and mailed with no envelope.

17. - PARIS - L'Opéra

PARIS OPERA. Of the billions of postcards sold during the Golden Age, many were bought with no intention of ever being mailed and headed straight into albums, as with this card. It is unwritten and has the telltale signs at the corners of a postcard that has spent years tucked into an album. A quote from *Macmillan's Magazine* 1904 draws the picture. "The delight in the collection of picture post-cards has grown to such a dimension that its extent would hardly be believed by those who have not had the opportunity to see it first hand." People were not awash in images as they would be only a few years later. Inexpensive postcards provided a view of the world that was a novelty in its time.

AVENUE DE L'OPÉRA. Note people walking casually down the avenue.

{
May 5, 1905
We are having delightful weather blue skies & brilliant sun.
The fashions here are gorgeous. —Will
}

Panorama du Trocadéro

PARIS WORLD'S FAIR OF 1900. View from the Eiffel Tower. In the distance, La Trocadero. Paris was famous for its World Fairs. The first one was held in 1855 and drew five million visitors. In 1867 the numbers grew to fifteen million. The fair of 1878, designed to show the world that France had recovered from its Civil War, drew sixteen million. 1889 was a celebration of the French Revolution and drew thirty-two million. The fair of 1900 attracted an astonishing fifty million people from around the world and lasted from May 6 to October 31. That is almost one million people a month in Paris. Imagine the shops, hotels, restaurants and cafés full to the brim.

143   PARIS. — Le Pont des Arts et l'Institut. — LL.

Paris in Color

While color photography existed as early as 1861, it was too expensive a process for the large numbers of postcards produced during the Golden Age. Thus the technique of the *pochoir*, or stencil art, was developed for the hand coloring of black and white views. Because tourism was a major engine driving the postcard industry, a majority of cards that were colored were of the most well traveled tourist spots in Paris, e.g., avenues, boulevards, monuments, etc. Given the importance of *pochoir* and the level of skill required to do it well, it is surprising that so little information exists on this art as applied to the postcard. The intricacy of the stencils, each cut by hand, and the detail in the application of the coloring are lost techniques.

70 PARIS (IXᵉ). — L'Opéra. — LL

PARIS OPERA. Designed by Charles Garnier. Completed in 1875. Garnier found the setting for his opera house too hemmed in by surrounding buildings. From some angles it looked like it was about to slip away, he said, and consequently he found himself leaning in the opposite direction as he approached. Many criticized his design for its garishness. He pointed out that this was a theatre, not a morgue. The nude figures on the sculpture of La Danse by Carpeaux on the opera steps brought cries of indignation and a splash of ink from an angry protestor.

*They do not allow us to send
tinseled postals through the mail.
We attended the theatre last evening
and saw grand opera. They were
playing Faust. To see the interior
alone is worth a trip to Paris.*

—*J. M. R.*

29. PARIS. ~ Place de l'Opéra

THE PARIS OPERA seen from Avenue de l'Opéra, all part of Haussmann's master plan for the modernization of Paris in the mid-19TH century. The opera house was inaugurated in 1875. This photo predates the opening of the Métro as there are no Métro entrances yet. On the left is the Grand Hotel with the Café de la Paix. The tinsel in the message refers to sparkle that was applied to lines of glue that had been laid down on the card. This postcard was mailed in an envelope.

June 17th
145 PARIS. — *Vue sur la Seine, prise du Pavillon de Flore.* - LL. Hotel St. Petersburg,
Have been in Paris since May 9th. Leave to day for London
for 3 weeks. Will go to Russia in July. also Denmark & Sweden.
Baden-Baden & Switzerland in August. Love to all, Cousin Belle

VIEW OF THE SEINE from atop the Louvre. In the distance, Notre–Dame. The two sides of this postcard are different colors. Postcards were printed on paper made up of three sheets of paper glued together. Green was often used for the message side because it was cheaper. This card was clearly collected and spent years glued in an album. The stamp was removed by a collector. Although not in color, this card is here because of the two cards that follow. Cousin Belle is enjoying a month-long trip in the grand old fashion. We don't know where she lived but we do know that she had loved ones in Berkeley, California. With three postcards dated 1905, 1906, and 1908, she either lived in Europe or traveled there often. Compare to next two pages.

CARTE POSTALE
Ce côté est exclusivement réservé à l'adresse

Mrs. W. S. Matthew
2009 Lincoln Street
Berkeley. California
États-Unis d'Amérique.

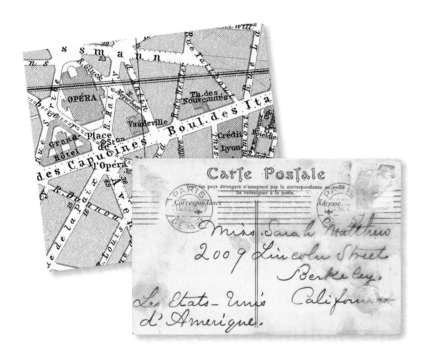

PARIS. — Le Grand Escalier de l'Opéra

GRAND STAIRCASE OF PARIS OPERA. Belle, like many Americans, was not yet familiar with the divided back postcard introduced earlier in France than in the U.S.

June 6 1908
165   PARIS. — *La Rue Soufflot et le Panthéon.* — LL.   With the love of Cousin Belle

RUE SOUFFLOT. From this perspective we know that the photographer was perched high on a ladder. The Pantheon was conceived by Louis XV as a church to commemorate Saint Genevieve, the patron saint of Paris. Its completion in 1790 was well timed for the Revolution. A year later it was nationalized. Twice again it became a church and twice it was descaralized. Today it stands as a national monument to the great men of France who are interred there. The original Rue Soufflot was laid out in 1760 as an approach to the new church then under construction. Haussmann tore that street down entirely to build this wider and longer street to connect with his Boulevard Saint-Michel. Compare to next page.

June 6, 1908
Dear Mamie,

I sent you a letter last night, and now send you a card of the Pantheon where the demonstration occurred. I wish I had a nearer view. The great heat we have experienced the past four days has left us and it is beautifully cool now—just right.
—Cousin Belle

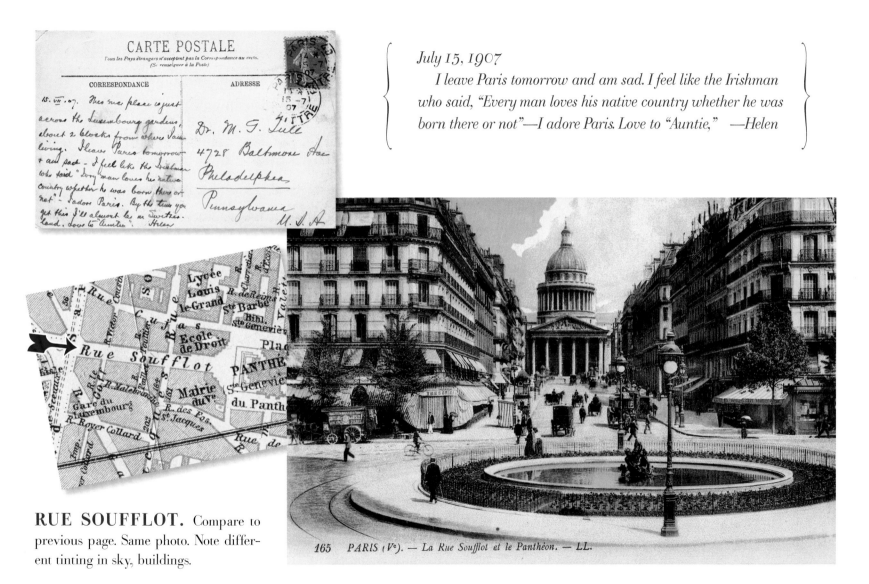

CARTE POSTALE

Tous les Pays étrangers n'acceptent pas la Correspondance au recto.
(Se renseigner à la Poste)

CORRESPONDANCE — ADRESSE

15. VII. '07. Mes ma place is just across the Luxembourg gardens, about 2 blocks from where I am living. I leave Paris tomorrow + am sad. I feel like the Irishman who said "Every man loves his native country whether he was born there or not" - I adore Paris. By the time you get this I'll almost be in Switzerland. Love to "Auntie." Helen

Dr. M. G. Lull
4728 Baltimore Ave
Philadelphia
Pennsylvania
U. S. A.

July 15, 1907

I leave Paris tomorrow and am sad. I feel like the Irishman who said, "Every man loves his native country whether he was born there or not"—I adore Paris. Love to "Auntie," —Helen

RUE SOUFFLOT. Compare to previous page. Same photo. Note different tinting in sky, buildings.

165 PARIS (V⁁). — La Rue Soufflot et le Panthéon. — LL.

(17)

PARIS. — La Tour Eiffel

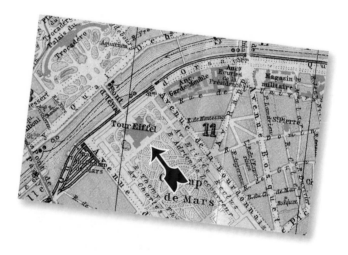

EIFFEL TOWER, designed by Gustave Eiffel for the Paris World's Fair of 1889. A marvel of modern technology, the tower was originally planned to stand only for the duration of the fair and then be dismantled. It was only saved after the government discovered the advantages of installing a telegraph station on the top. In the distance is the Trocadero. Note postmark from atop the tower.

My Dear Sis,

Hello honey, how are you today? Gee I hope you are just fine and dandy. I do not feel so good today but hope to be OK in a short time. —*Goodbye Sis as ever Buddie*

EIFFEL TOWER. It took a phone call to the Springfield, Ohio Historical Society to decipher the address on this card and to learn that Buddie is actually Rudolph. At home he was a bricklayer. His parents were Adolphe and Maggie. His sister Anna was a seamstress. His other sister Lucy was a bookbinder. A brother William was a clerk. Buddie wrote this card in 1918 while in the military with the American Expeditionary Forces. The stamp tells us that the card passed the censors. The postcard already shows signs of a decline in quality. While few postcards are perfectly squared, nothing is aligned here. The card is almost a parallelogram instead of a rectangle, and the Eiffel Tower is not aligned to the card edges or the text.

110   PARIS. — La Conciergerie. — LL.

THE CONCIERGERIE, on right, was begun in the Middle Ages and was originally a royal palace. It later became a prison. During the Revolution it housed the tribunal where several thousand were condemned and carted away to the guillotine. Marie Antoinette spent her last days here. Today it is a complex of law courts. The Tribunal de Commerce on the left is also a law court and was built by Haussmann.

250   PARIS. — Le Parc Monceau — LL.

PARC MONCEAU. This park was originally established in the 1770s by the Duke of Orleans, cousin of Louis XVI. At the Revolution, to show that he was one of the people, the Duke abandoned his title of nobility to become Philippe Egalité and turned on his cousin the King by signing his death warrant. This served little purpose, for the Duke lost his head on the scaffold in 1793. The park was made state property and was later returned to the Duke's descendents in 1815. It was acquired by the city in 1852 and entirely redone by Haussmann in 1861.

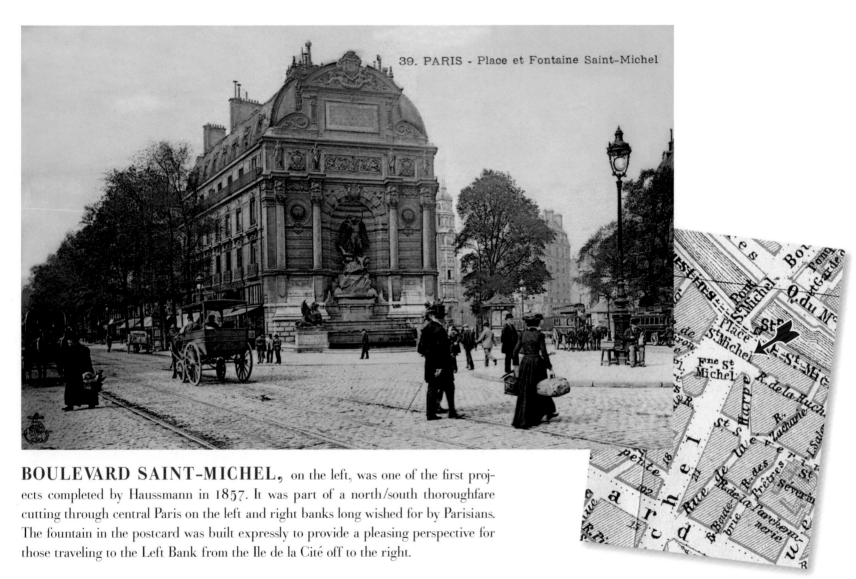

39. PARIS - Place et Fontaine Saint-Michel

BOULEVARD SAINT-MICHEL, on the left, was one of the first projects completed by Haussmann in 1857. It was part of a north/south thoroughfare cutting through central Paris on the left and right banks long wished for by Parisians. The fountain in the postcard was built expressly to provide a pleasing perspective for those traveling to the Left Bank from the Ile de la Cité off to the right.

March 24, 1910

 Received all letters & papers at Paris. Enjoying very much, weather bad, but we see a great many people on the boulevards and last night went to see Faust at the grand Opera House. It is very beautiful, were then at Maxims till 3 a.m. and are today on the bum. Had bubbles which accounts for the bumness. Are now eating dinner at Vienna Café on Boulevard des Italiens. —*Love to all, M… & Will*

FONTAINE SAINT-MICHEL. Designed by Gabrielle Davioud and inaugurated on August 15, 1860. Today an icon of the Left Bank, this fountain with the Archangel Michael slaying the dragon was poorly received in its time. A verse of the day conveys the sentiment. "In this execrable monument, one sees neither talent or taste. The Devil is worth nothing. Saint-Michel is not worth the Devil."

22   PARIS. — NOTRE-DAME.   D. L.

July 4, 1904
Kind Friend,

    I am in Paris today. Yesterday I was on the Battle Field of
Waterloo and saw where the greatest of all generals was defeated.
Brussels is a beautiful city and I found Berlin a beautiful city of
splendour but I think Paris will have to be the most splendid city
in Europe. Hope you are well.   *—G. W. Biersbom*

NOTRE-DAME. The first stone was laid in 1163. For hundreds of years
the cathedral retained its original light coloring, until the advent of the automobile,
when it began to blacken from exhaust fumes. In the 1960s, Minister of Culture
André Malraux began a major project to clean all Paris monuments and restore them
to their original color. In about 2000 the cathedral was cleaned again.

November 3, 1913

We are so near this beautiful arch that we see it often. You would be surprised at the kind of breakfast they serve at the best hotels, or rather you would not call it a breakfast at all. In the swellest places it is nothing but a couple of hard rolls and coffee. In some others you get honey and jam therewith but in the best ones you pay extra.

—O. J. S.

8 PARIS (VIIIᵉ). — L'Arc de Triomphe. -- LL

THE ARC DE TRIOMPHE was commissioned by Napoleon I to celebrate his victory at the Battle of Austerlitz. Construction began in 1808 and was completed in 1836. Built as a symbol of French victory, years later, in 1871, at the end of the Franco-Prussian War, the arch became a symbol of defeat when the Prussian army marched underneath and down the Champs Elysées. Once the Germans left Paris the French poured gasoline on the avenue and set it ablaze to purge the noxious spirits.

PARIS. — L'Arc-de-Triomphe et les Champs-Elysées. — LL.

ARC DE TRIOMPHE AND THE CHAMPS-ELYSÉES. An English traveler of 1847 describes this avenue: "It is difficult to conceive a more lively scene than this walk affords on a fine evening, and more particularly on a Sunday. Gaiety of every description is going on, and almost every sound vibrates on the ear." Until the 1960s the avenue was the height of fashion, sophistication and elegance. In recent years it has struggled with a loss of identity as the influx of fast food restaurants and chain stores has rendered it banal.

October 7, 1906
Finally landed in gay
Paris. This is where every-
one drives in the afternoon.
If you don't own an auto,
jump in a taxicab.
—Fred & Katie

June 3, 1911

We are still in Gay Paree. Leave in a week for London and will leave for home about 24TH of June. It is awfully close here. You get so tired there is not much pleasure trying to get around. The shops are stifling. Had a great storm yesterday, but is just as warm today.

—Louise

4069. PARIS - Avenue des Champs-Élysées

CHAMPS-ELYSÉES. In the message we see the phrase "gay paree." This came into use in the late 19TH century to describe the merriment of naughty Paris and was common in song lyrics, novels, magazine articles and everyday parlance. The phrase has come back into use in recent years but with a different spin.

2 *PARIS (VIII°). — L'Avenue des Champs-Élysées. — LL.*

CHAMPS-ELYSÉES. The name of this avenue derives from the Elysian Fields, a region in the Greek underworld where blessed souls chosen by the gods found their final resting place. From its origins in the 17TH century until about 1800, this was largely a pastoral scene of elm trees and pathways for strolling and riding during the day but to be avoided at night. In 1828 the state ceded the Champs-Elysées to the city and with this came sidewalks, gas lamps, restaurants, cafés, theatres and other amenities to draw a public seeking diversion in elegant surroundings.

June 18, 1910

Paris is surely a wonderful city. I should like to spend a month here some time. We go to London tomorrow. We shall probably be there for the King's funeral.

—R.B.E.

August 26, 1909
Dear Aunt Sophia,
*   I will look for you in N.Y.*
Be shure and come. We are
going to the country in the
morning.
*   —Your loving nephew,*
*   Chas*

AVENUE DE LA GRANDE ARMEÉ. Here in western Paris, beyond the Arc de Triomphe, the well heeled enjoy a Sunday stroll and gather around one of the new automobiles to be seen on Paris streets.

431 PARIS. — *L'Avenue du Bois de Boulogne.* — LL.

AVENUE DU BOIS DE BOULOGNE. While in exile in London, Napoleon III greatly admired Hyde Park and wanted to create something as beautiful for Paris. The Bois de Boulogne was one of the first projects he got underway upon taking power in 1853. Haussmann completed the massive project in 1858 after planting 200,000 trees and laying down sixty miles of new roadway. It became the fashion to stroll on this avenue on a Sunday afternoon to watch all the fine carriages returning from the horse races at Longchamp. Many arranged chairs at the curb to watch the passing show, as seen in this photo.

431 PARIS. – L'Avenue du Bois de Boulogne. – LL.

AVENUE DU BOIS DE BOULOGNE. Same photo as preceding page; two different treatments of hand tinting.

542. - PARIS. - Place de la République

PLACE DE LA RÉPUBLIQUE. Created by Haussmann between 1856 and 1865. One of the most common criticisms leveled against Haussmann is that the motive behind his transformation of Paris was the military advantage the new city provided the government in times of social uprising. It is no accident that on this square linking eight major thoroughfares fanning out across Paris, he built an army barracks housing 3,000 troops who could easily be deployed in any direction along ramrod straight avenues and boulevards. The barracks are seen here behind the statue.

June 15, 1910

Dear Bro. Squires,

Nearly two weeks away and not a word. I wonder what you are thinking of me. Really Leo. you can't tell how I miss the companionship of you fellows. So I'm coming back in a week or two and my sister with me. If you are like me Paris will be a big disappointment as far as their famous women are concerned. It is a bigger city and busier but oh how dirty and loose everything is. I like you Paris but oh you Berlin. My sister and old maids send best regards … We are going to the opera tonight. This is the place to see Paris gowns and Paris women at their very best. Havn't been to Moulin Rouge or any bad place yet, but don't want to go. Have lost the lust. Auf Baldiges Weidersehn.

—Great all saints and friends for me, Dean

PARIS (XVIᵉ). — L'AVENUE DU BOIS DE BOULOGNE.

AVENUE DU BOIS DE BOULOGNE.

182. – PARIS. – Le Guignol des Champs-Elysées

PUPPET SHOW ON THE CHAMPS-ELYSÉES. A common reprimand made to children in France is *"Arrête de faire le Guignol!"* Stop clowning around! Guignol is the main character in the French version of the Punch & Judy show, created around 1800 by a dentist in Lyon who tried puppetry as a way to attract new clients. It worked so well that he gave up dentistry and for generations his descendents carried on the family tradition. Originally full of ascerbic wit and biting humor and intended for adults, this was not the feel good entertainment contemporary audiences would expect from a puppet show. Over time it has taken on a tone more palatable for young audiences. A 1912 Paris guide describes a theater dedicated to Guignol on Rue Chaptal and warns againt taking "the young, the nervous, or the easily shocked." These were puppets with attitude and productions were full of coffins, guillotines and scenes of torture.

40   PARIS. — Le Petit Palais — LL

THE PETIT PALAIS. Stands across the street from the Grand Palais, and like it was built for the World's Fair of 1900. Today it is an art museum.

875 PARIS (VIII°). — Le Pont Alexandre III. — LL.

PONT ALEXANDER III. This bridge was constructed for the 1900 Paris World's Fair to symbolize a new Franco-Russian alliance and was named after Russian Emperor Alexander III. The first stone was laid in 1896 with President Félix Faure and Czar Nicholas II present. This is the same Czar who was assassinated in 1918 along with his wife and family during the Bolshevik Revolution.

June 27, 1911
Tell your mother that father has crossed this bridge. I see a great many nice little French babies just about as big as you & they all seem to be good little girls. —"Father"

218

PARIS. — Perspective du Pont Alexandre III

Collections ND Phot

PONT ALEXANDER III from the Right Bank. In the distance, the Grand Palais. A Sunday afternoon of strolling. One of the designs submitted for this bridge was of reinforced concrete. A new building technique, and as yet unproven, it was rejected for the single span steel bridge seen here.

15   PARIS (VIII)ᵉ. — La Madeleine et la Rue Royale.   D. L.

Miss K. D. Root
Georgetown
U.S.A.
Mass.

RUE ROYALE AND LA MADELEINE. In 1763 Louis XV commissioned architect Constant d'Ivry to design a church for this site. When d'Ivry died during construction, the new architect razed everything and designed a new church based on the Roman Pantheon. All work came to a halt with the Revolution. In 1806, Napoleon I cleared the site once again and began to erect a memorial to honor his military. His fall from power left the project unfinished. After the completion of the Arc de Triomphe in 1836, another monument glorifying the Grand Armée seemed excessive and the future of this spot became uncertain. Some argued for a train station, a bank or a library. Louis XVIII completed the work in 1842 and consecrated the site as a church dedicated to Mary Magdalene.

We are having a great time all the time—Weather is perfect and we both are feeling better—Paris is "one gay place"

—Lyman

Flora went abroad
Lovely little fraud
On her way
Ran far away
And caused much

Consternation as she
Roved the sea
Over the countree
Near and far
Eating and drinking
Merry and shrinking
Into cathedrals and
Lovely old lands
Looking for beauty
Entering into everything
Return here soon

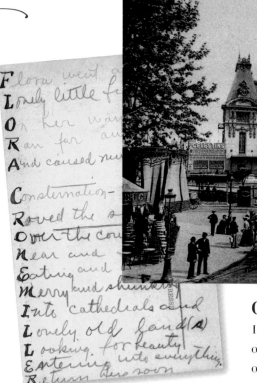

GARE DE LYON. On Right Bank. Originally built between 1847–1852 and entirely rebuilt and enlarged for the World's Fair of 1900. A restaurant in the station, Le Train Bleu, is a classic of its time, richly decorated and ornamented. The message on this postcard has a story. The rhyme is forced but makes its point. Little Flora Cronemiller is in trouble, a runaway. We wish her well.

214. — PARIS. —
La Place de l'Opéra avec le Grand Hôtel.

A. Riant, éditeur.

THE GRAND HOTEL ON PLACE DE L'OPÉRA. The Café de la Paix with the red striped awning wraps around the corner. Compare to pages 78, 80, and 81. On the left is the Boulevard des Capucines. It was on that boulevard in 1895, at number 14 in the basement of the Grand Café, that the Lumiere brothers projected the first motion pictures for a paying audience. The press were invited but saw little value in the invention and did not attend. The brothers made a rental agreement with the café owner, Volpini, for one year and offered him 20% of the receipts. Volpini refused and demanded 30 francs a night. The success of the novelty was immediate and the owner had a long time to regret his decision.

73. PARIS – Jardin des Tuileries

TUILERIES GARDENS. These gardens were laid out in 1664 by royal landscape gardener André Le Nôtre. An earlier, smaller garden had been created here in 1564 by Catherine de Medici for her Tuileries Palace. When her astrologer Ruggieri told her that she would die near Saint-Germain, she fled and built another palace near Les Halles because this spot was in the parish of Saint-Germain l'Auxxerois. In 1589, while touring the countryside, she fell ill in Blois. A Bishop was called to her aid. "What is your name?" she asked. "Saint-Germain" was the reply. She died the next day.

April 20. About 6 minutes from 18 bis. The famous Patisserie where Nevis and I treat ourselves to the famous "Coquelin bombe" which consist of a cream made of pounded chestnuts. vanilla, sugar, almin, this "Yo-frosting-flavor. Does-your-mouth water? Next door is-where I buy-ham. etc.

RUE AND PLACE PASSY. The bakery mentioned in the message is in the white building. Until 1860 Passy was a village outside of Paris described as "charming, remarkable for its salubrious air, extensive views and delightful villas." Benjamin Franklin chose Passy as his residence during his nine years in France. In the 1820s two coach companies competed for the business of transporting people to Paris from this place. When one gained the favor of the Mayor of Passy and he prohibited the other from entering his village, the director of the latter threw himself into the Canal Saint Martin. Off to the right today, just out of the frame, is a McDonald's.

April 20, 1907

About 6 minutes from 18 bis is the famous Patisserie where … and I treat ourselves to the famous "Coquelin bombe." which consists of a cream made of pounded chestnuts, vanilla, sugar, eggs and flavored with alum. This is covered with a frosting. Does your mouth water? Next door is where I buy ham, etc.

January 9, 1904
Mr. Leon Liebes
1814 Pacific Avenue
San Francisco, California

My Dear Leon,
*   I think this is such a*
pretty postal. I hope uncle
Phillip is getting along
nicely. Write me soon.
*   —Lots of love to all,*
*   Aunt Flora*

126. PARIS — Parc Montsouris - Les Allées   C.L.C.

PARC MONTSOURIS. This is an unusual card. A close-up of people with no one posing or even acknowledging the camera is most uncommon. Postcards were printed twenty or thirty to a sheet and cut on a machine. At the top of this card we see that the cutter that day was not paying attention.

205. — PARIS. — Place des Victoires et la Rue Etienne Marcel. — *A. R.*

PLACE DES VICTOIRES. Constructed in the 17TH century as a monument to Louis XIV, whose statue stands in the center. The street going off into the distance is Rue Etienne Marcel, begun in 1858 by Haussmann and intended to cut all the way through the Marais to Boulevard Beaumarchais. Instead it stops at Rue Beaubourg.

*Here's where
Jeanette bought her
opera coat—at last!
She can now be
dressed up drunk
and highly perfumed.
—Beans*

RUE AUBER. On left, Grand Hotel with
Café de la Paix. On right, Garnier opera house.

THE PANTHEON. The only thing remarkable about this unremarkable post-card is the address.

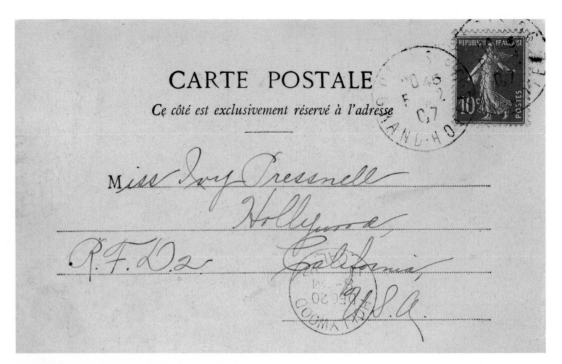

In 1907 Hollywood was a small town of 3,415, one half hour by train from Los Angeles. Note the address, RFD2. Rural Free Delivery was established in 1896 to deliver mail to remote farm communities across America.

Sparsely built with a hotel, bank, church, library, and high school, much of Hollywood was still open ranch land with large lemon and orange groves. A 1903 ordinance prohibited herding more than 200 cattle through town streets. Miss Presnell most likely went to a general store to pick up her postcard.

Because of a lack of water, Hollywood was annexed to Los Angeles in 1910. The vote among Angelinos was 6,624 for and 373 against. The first movie studio was built in 1911 in an old tavern. Ten years later the city was unrecognizable.

Paris in Black & White

Of the thousands of views of Paris that were photographed for postcards, the great majority were produced in black and white. Hand tinted postcards were done mostly of the well touristed areas: the boulevards, monuments, etc. These certainly have their appeal, as these pages demonstrate. But the black and whites, when well done, are priceless. More so when we know that the photographer could not simply snap away and then choose the best shot. Setting up the bulky wooden ladder and mounting the camera was no small task. Changing the glass plate after each shot made the process most cumbersome. Then there was framing the photo and choosing the right time of day for the right light. Photographers are always chasing the light. And the waiting. The photographer did not want anyone or anything too close to him. So he waited for the buggy to pass, or the crowd to open up to make a more pleasing tableau.

Having done two books on Paris, I know these difficulties. And today it is even more arduous with all the things that can spoil a view: crowds of people, cars, large tourist buses, green refuse containers in front of every door on a street. Photographing Paris is as difficult as photographing animals in nature. You must know your territory, and above all you must know how to wait.

My advice to anyone going to Paris in the summer: Wake up at the crack of dawn on a Sunday morning. Walk to Notre-Dame to see the cathedral in the early light. Then stroll along the Seine as the city slowly awakens. There are no cars, no crowds. It is quiet. The colors of the early light are muted. It is almost Paris in black and white.

57 PARIS. - Place et Fontaine Saint-Michel.

FONTAINE SAINT-MICHEL. This is a remarkably quiet photo of Place Saint-Michel—a Left Bank hub. A horse drawn omnibus makes a stop on its way from La Chapelle to Square Monge. The omnibus in the distance waits to begin its run to Trocadero. A man in a top hat reads a newspaper while waiting. Corners speak of years in an album.

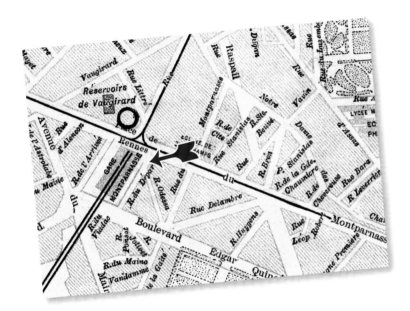

PARIS..Accident de la Gare Montparnasse
(21 octobre 1895). ND

ACCIDENT AT THE GARE MONTPARNASSE. October 21, 1895. The one fatality was a flower seller sitting below. Accidents, catastrophes and acts of God were prime subjects for postcards.

CRUE DE LA SEINE
Paris — Rue Bonaparte — 29 Janvier 1910

RUE BONAPARTE. The Great Flood of 1910. This street leads to the church of Saint-Germain des Pres. For several hundred years this church was at the center of a large, walled abbey surrounded by a moat. Water for the moat was drawn from the Seine along a deep channel that, once filled, became this street. Seen here, the street recaptures its original character. Message on front of the card, "Look at the pavement floating about. Paris is a wreck."

February 15, 1910

Hello Josie, and thanks for the Christmas card. How would you like to be here now? It is very exciting, but a little wet. You must be having a dandy winter.

—Give P. my love.

With love, S.G.

CRUE DE LA SEINE PARIS - Rue de Bièvre
Le 30 Janvier 1910

RUE DE BIEVRE. The Great Flood of 1910. This neighborhood was one of the poorer in central Paris and in the 1920s was tagged a slum to be torn down and rebuilt. It was saved by individuals with imagination who fought for its preservation and restoration. Today it is one of the most exclusive streets in Paris. President Mitterand ended his days here.

470 PARIS. — L'Avenue du Bois de Boulogne. — Retour des Courses. — LL. *Oct 8th 1900*

AVENUE DU BOIS DE BOLOGNE. The sidewalk is thick with crowds watching the carriages returning from the racetrack at Longchamps. Many have brought chairs and arrive early to get prime seats for the passing spectacle. Compare to pages 30, 31, and 33.

October 8, 1900
This is the well known avenue! Irma and I walk here every morning for about an hour. We live about where the cross is on the other side of the arch!

443. PARIS — Rue Saint-Dominique - La Fontaine de Mars . G. B. R. R.

RUE SAINT-DOMINIQUE. This site in the 7TH arrondisement is remarkably intact today. When the aristocracy abandoned the Marais in the early 17TH century, it was to this neighborhood that they moved and built many grand houses designed by France's greatest architects. The eastern portion of this street (off to the right) was amputated by Haussmann for his new Boulevard Saint-Germain. Many aristocratic residences were lost, among them the stately Hotel De Luynes. A marble staircase with muralled walls was so spectacular that the whole was preserved and now stands in the Carnavalet Museum to remind us of a lost grandeur.

FOUNTAIN AND PLACE SAINT-MICHEL. On the right, a bus with an open platform on the back. Great fun to ride, now gone from Paris streets.

September 8, 1911
Mother dear;

It is from this "place" that I take the bus to go across the river for mail. The one at the right shows the kind. We go early Sunday a.m. to the sea-shore for a few days. It is quite near here. Got Fr's letter. Tell him to send me the "Breeze" regularly. Am writing these days and studying hard. Love to you all. Give me o.c.o. address.

—Lovingly,
Ann

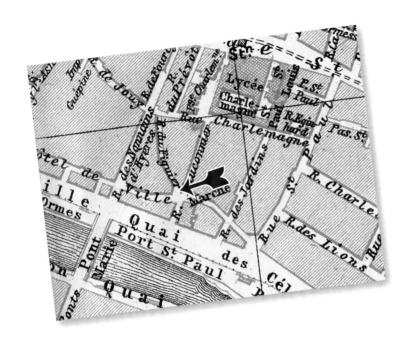

HOTEL DE SENS. One of the few medieval buildings remaining in Paris. Completed in 1519 as a residence for the Archbishops of Sens on their visits to the capital. When Paris received its own Archbishop in 1623, the site fell into private hands and degraded over the years. It housed a variety of enterprises including a stagecoach inn, boarding house, marmalade factory, and as pictured here, a glass making factory. The hotel was bought by the city in 1911. Restoration was completed in 1951. Today it houses the Forney Library. On the very left is a large market hall built in 1878 and torn down along with the building on the extreme right in different phases of the quarter's evolution.

174 PARIS. — L'Hôtel de Sens. — LL.

L. J. & Cⁱᵉ, édit., Angoulême-Paris

Paris Historique. — 60. Vieux Montmartre, la rue Saint-Rustique

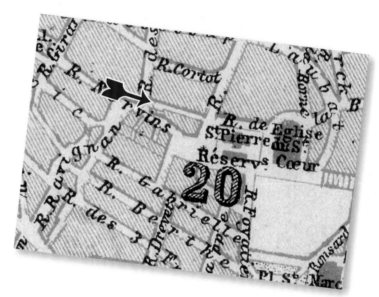

RUE SAINT-RUSTIQUE. *Detail.* This tiny street on the hill in Montmartre began as a footpath in the 11TH century. In 1867 Haussmann announced plans to widen the street to thirty-six feet to put a major thoroughfare through Montmartre, effectively erasing the street from the map. This was one of many of his plans never carried out. In the distance, Église Sacré Coeur.

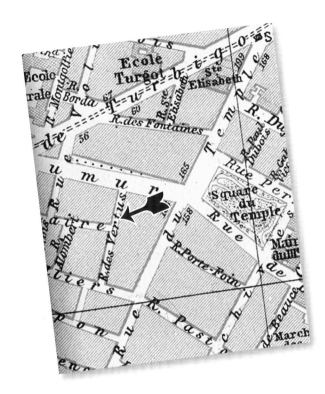

82. — Vieil hotel, dit du Puits de Rome
Cour de Rome, rue des Vertus

RUE DES VERTUS. Street of Virtues. It is thought that this street received its name as a compensation for a particular type of young girl who lived here. Two workmen in a courtyard take a moment to pause for posterity.

191. - RUELLE SOURDIS et RUE
de BEAUCE. Ouverte en 1626, au fond rue de Bretagne.

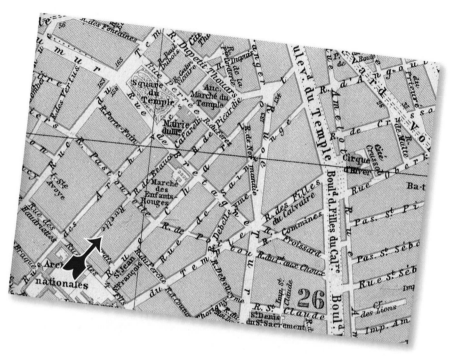

RUELLE SOURDIS AND RUE DE BEAUCE, created in
1626. Nothing has changed here. Ruelle Sourdis in the foreground is today a
private way closed off at the end by a gate installed in 1832. Its continuation,
Rue de Beauce, was to be widened once in 1799 to nineteen feet, and a second
time in 1835 to thirty-two feet. Neither was carried out, and today the street is
as narrow as it was in 1626.

G. C. A. Paris

517. MONTMARTRE — Place du Tertre (coin Norvins)

PLACE DU TERTRE. Montmartre. Anyone who has visited Paris knows that this charming square and the streets around it are intact but have become a tourist mecca. The best way to see anything resembling this photo is in the early morning when all is quiet and no one is in sight.

PARIS. — LE PONT NEUF

A. Taride, Paris

PONT NEUF. Completed 1605. This was the first bridge built across the Seine with no houses on it. Until then all bridges were lined end to end with houses and shops. Anyone crossing a bridge had no sense of leaving the land. The Pont Neuf gave a view of the river no Parisian had ever seen and made this a most popular place of promenade. The crowds were so great that it brought about the invention of sidewalks and curbs to protect people from passing carriages. The building on the right in the distance is La Belle Jardiniere. Compare to next page.

29. PARIS — Rue du Pont-Neuf et Samaritaine   C. L. C.

RUE DU PONT NEUF. This street was created by Haussmann between 1854–1867 as a link between the Seine and the central markets, Les Halles. On the right is the department store La Belle Jardiniere which moved here in 1866 from its original location on Ile de la Cité. In the middle, La Samaritaine. The two buildings on the left were later torn down when La Samaritaine needed larger quarters to expand. Compare to previous page.

RUE SAINT-ANDRÉ DES ARTS. Townhouse built in 1740. Barely visible over the street sign on the facade is a much older street sign with the word "Saint" scratched out during the anti-clerical fervor of the Revolution. Hundreds of years ago, this street and Rue de la Huchette were a continuous footpath through a vineyard.

Les Grands Boulevards

*T*he boulevards, known as Les Grands Boulevards, were created by Louis XIV on the line of old ramparts that encircled the city on the north. Several miles in length, they extend in a semi-circle from Place de la Bastille to the Madeleine. Originally located at the edge of the city, this became a popular tree-lined promenade for the nobility who sought distraction in the clean air of the country. In time, cafés, restaurants, cabarets and clubs established here to cater to the leisure class. A distinction in the boulevards—eastern portions is working class, the western portion is for the wealthy—reflects the larger layout of Paris. East is poor, West is monied. The most fashionable and popular stretch of boulevard for many years were the Boulevards des Italiens and des Capucines. For habitués of the finer things in life to be had there, to venture eastward to the Boulevard St. Denis and beyond was tantamount to leaving the civilized world. In the 19TH century, the Boulevard du Temple, located around today's Place de la Republique, was known as the Boulevard of Crime. The working class flocked to the numerous theaters located there featuring presentations of murder and mayhem. The area is well portrayed in the film *The Children of Paradise.*

1198 PARIS. — La Madeleine et le Boulevard de la Madeleine. — LL.

LA MADELEINE AND BOULEVARD DE LA MADELEINE. In

1847 a massive funeral was held here for grand courtesan Marie Duplessis. See next page.
Chopin's funeral was held here in 1849. Note address on postcard. No street number. Everyone
knew everyone.

Honey Dear:

I am just too homesick to stay on therefore am leaving on the 6th. I shall be in Buffalo about Jan. I & then will see you & tell you all I have seen, done, meet, etc. I shall be glad to get home. I am thinking of you a lot even if I don't write.

—Heaps of love always,

Anne W.

Champs-Elysées 62; *Nathan*, Rue Scribe 3 (the las
Swann, Rue de Castiglione 12 (American).
CHOCOLATE, TEA, etc.: *Compagnie Coloniale, A
Marquis*, Passage des Panoramas 57–61; *Au Fidè
Boul. de la Madeleine 9; *Guérin - Boutron &
nière 29; *Masson*, Rue de Rivoli 91. See also
CIGARS. The manufacture and sale of tol
naire' and '*supérieur*') and cigars is a mono
The shops, called *débits de la régie des tabacs*,
their red lamps. The prices are the same ever
American tobacco may be obtained at various
Rivoli, the boulevards, and other streets frequ
the principal depot, Quai d'Orsay 63, at the Place
Good imported cigars (25 c. each, and upward
St. Honoré 157 ('A la Civette'), or at the Grand-H
on the open boxes) of the home-made cigars us

783 *PARIS. — Le Boulevard de la Madeleine. —* LL.

BOULEVARD DE LA MADELEINE. Grand courtesan Marie Duplessis lived on this boulevard at number 15. Born into poverty in Normandy, she was sold by her father at age fifteen and brought
to Paris. Intelligent, attractive, with great refinement and a quick wit, she went from holding menial jobs to
becoming one of the great courtesans of her time. Among her lovers were Alexander Dumas and Franz List.
She was the inspiration for the figure of Camille in *La Dame aux Camelias* and for Violetta in *La Traviata*.
She died in her sumptuous apartment here in 1847 at age twenty-three.

372 PARIS. — Le Boulevard des Italiens. — LL.

BOULEVARD DES ITALIENS. Compare this postcard to next page. Note details, e.g., time on clock is 10:15 AM, policeman standing on island, delivery man at curb on left with his cart open as he organizes for a delivery. On the right a man pushes another cart down the street. Note coach drawn by three horses coming down the street. The photographer is perched high on a ladder in the middle of the boulevard.

June 15, 1908
Dear Babe,
    This is one of the liveliest boulevards in Paris. You should have your pony here and ride out to the Bois de Boulogne each day. It is very fashionable.
                    —Lovingly,
                M. E. Hesselgrave

372 PARIS (IXe). — Le Boulevard des Italiens. — LL.

BOULEVARD DES ITALIENS. Compare to previous postcard. This is the same photo but has been seriously retouched with early Photoshop. Time on clock is the same, 10:15 AM, as are the policeman under the clock, the delivery man on left at curb. But coming down the street, that green and yellow vehicle is a bus. Early photo retouching techniques allowed easy manipulation of images by superimposing negatives. The bus was added most likely to modernize the postcard. Find other differences. On next page, note clock at 10:25 AM. Same day, same shoot ten minutes later. Note different treatment of awnings on right.

372. PARIS. — Le Boulevard des Italiens. — LL.

BOULEVARD DES ITALIENS. Compare to previous postcard. Same day, same photographer, ten minutes later. Note different treatment of awnings on right. One of the most famous boulevardiers of the early 19TH century was Nestor Roqueplan. A great epicure, he offered two pieces of advice to friends. One: Never eat mushrooms during times of social unrest because the food inspectors at Les Halles always grow lax in their duties. Two: Only eat the middle section of the baguette because the *porteurs* always leave them standing in a corner, making them easy targets for passing dogs.

June 23, 1911

*We think of the dear wife
& little ones often and trust all
are well. We are gradually working towards Engld thence to N.Y.
& Boston & hope to arrive in dear
Cal^a early in August. We
are both well, and enjoying
our hurried sightseeing.*

—Sincerely, Uncle John

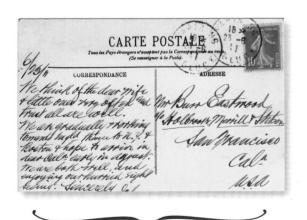

257. - PARIS. - Boulevard des Capucines, vue prise de la Chaussée d'Antin

BOULEVARD DES CAPUCINES. View taken from Chaussée d'Antin.

588. - PARIS. - Boulevard des Italiens - Carrefour Drouot

BOULEVARD DES ITALIENS looking west towards the Carrefour Drouot. This intersection was greatly altered when Boulevard Haussmann was cut through around 1926. The building with the dome still stands. The buildings behind the trees on the left were demolished. Note map and Boulevard Haussmann stopping at Rue Taitbout before it was extended to the boulevard.

October 30, 1908
  Went to the opera Faust Monday night. Best ever. 150 pieces in orchestra. Never dreamed that music could so effect one so much. Having a fine time. Wish all our good friends were here.

Fromage (à la crème) *Suisse* or *Gervais*, *Coeur*, cream-cheese. *Fromage de Gruyère*, Gruyère cheese. *Fromage de Roquefort*, made of a mixture of sheep's milk and goat's milk. Brie, *Camembert*, *Neufchâtel*, *Pont l'Évêque*, kinds of cheese made in Normandy.

15. WINES.

The following are a few of the finer wines :— Red Bordeaux or Claret: *St. Emilion* and *St. Julien* (2½-4 fr.), *Château Larose*, *Ch. Latour*, and *Ch. Laffitte* (7-10 fr.). White Bor—

The bread of Paris is excellent and h

68 PARIS. — *Le Boulevard des Italiens et le Café Riche*. — LL.

BOULEVARD DES ITALIENS AND THE CAFÉ RICHE, one of the most expensive restaurants on the boulevard, catering to writers and musicans of note. Henri Murger, author of the serialized novel *Scènes de la Vie de Bohème*, later to become the opera *La Boheme*, began his career as a starving artist at the Café Momus near the Louvre, where he and his destitute friends were known as the Water Drinkers. One would order a coffee, the others sipped water. With Murger's success came money and dinners at the Café Riche. This building was torn down. A large bank stands in its place.

1401   PARIS (X°). — Le Boulevard Bonne-Nouvelle. — LL.

BOULEVARD BONNE-NOUVELLE. *Actual size.* Created 1680-1685. Much
of Paris has been leveled during the course of its evolution, either to build some areas higher or
to lower others. A hill ran along the entire length of the south side of this boulevard (right) and
was leveled during the winter of 1709. Paris was undergoing a winter of sub-zero temperatures
with near-famine conditions and high unemployment. To help the working class, 15,000 were
hired to carry out the project.

August 26, 1909
  Dear Grandpa and Grandma,
I will soon be at home and
Grandma would you please
make me some cold slaw. And
Grandpa you will soon have a
boy to follow you.
  —Your grandson, C.O.S.

PARIS — Boulevard Bonne-Nouvelle

BOULEVARD BONNE-NOUVELLE. The difference in level on the left is a vestige of old Paris when a fortification ran along here, part of a defensive system on the Right Bank.

104 PARIS. — *Le Boulevard Saint-Denis.* — LL.

BOULEVARD SAINT-DENIS WITH PORTE SAINT-DENIS. This gate was built in 1672 on what was then the edge of the city. Its purpose was to add to the pomp and circumstance of a monarch's entry into Paris. To the left of the gate on the outside of the city were fruit orchards and vegetable gardens. Queen Victoria was the last monarch to pass through this gate on her visit to Paris in 1855 for the first Paris World's Fair. Compare to next page—same photo tinted differently. Note different treatment of sky.

104   PARIS. — Le Boulevard Saint-Denis.

BOULEVARD SAINT-DENIS WITH PORTE SAINT-DENIS.

Compare to previous page. In the late 19TH century, at number 23 in the boulevard, stood the Café Chartreuse, a repair for out of work musicians. It must have done a brisk business.

4009. PARIS
Boulevard des Italiens

BOULEVARD DES ITALIENS. Off in the distance, on the right, the Garnier opera house.

The Café Life

ard to imagine today, but one of the most novel experiences for an American traveling to Paris, even into the 1970s, was a visit to a café with outdoor seating where one could sit for hours with a single drink and do nothing more than watch the world go by. The introduction of espresso coffee in America in the late 1950s brought with it the creation of the café, and while it has grown, it has never taken off as in Europe. For all the Americans who emulate the lifestyle of the south of France or Italian Tuscany and fill their houses with Mediterranean colors, the right olive oil, furniture, and knickknacks, all intended to evoke the life of Provence—the one thing missing, the key to that slow paced, more pleasurable life is the café. Go to the café!

BOULEVARD DES CAPUCINES AND THE CAFÉ DE LA PAIX. Note sign on left for Les Dolly Sisters. These were twin sisters, born in Hungary, who emigrated to America in 1905 and became a star dancing duo on the vaudeville circuit. They were equally successful in Europe, as this sign shows. To boost ticket sales they took on other partners and created pseudo rivalries. Their lives ended tragically: one committed suicide; the other tried and failed.

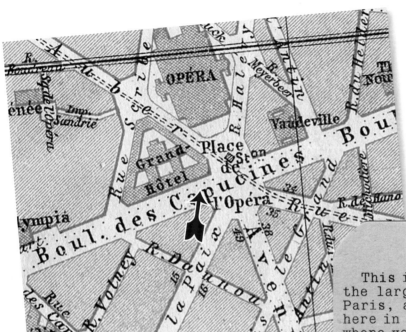

This is a picture of the famous Cafe de la Paix, one of
the largest and most centrally located restaurants in
Paris, and known around the World. It is the fashion,
here in Paris, not to take your coffee at the restaurant
where you eat your lunch or dinner, but to go to another
restaurant, usually to one with chairs and tables on the
side walk (outside terrace) and there take your coffee.
It is a pleasing custom and I myself enjoy doing it.

   Prices in Paris restaurants are not high - sixty cents
buys a good dinner at an ordinary place, but at the Cafe
de Paris (the most expensive place here) seven dollars
is nearer the price. At Maxims Cafe a dish of sliced
peaches costs a dollar and a half, but if you eat at
Maxims you eat in '' gay luxury '' and you must pay for
the Maxim atmosphere.

   When you come to Paris, see me because I have some
wonderful Paris addresses and sight-seeing information
for you.

                         Alden Scott Boyer
                                President.

Pastry Cooks.

The *Pâtissiers* rely mainly upon the sale of their goods for c... ...mption elsewhere; the customers who frequent them in the af... ...ons to enjoy their 'goûter' (cakes and pastry) are chiefly la... children. The most celebrated *Pâtisseries* are the followi... ...*art* (Julien jeune), Boul. des Italiens 9, corner of Rue Fav... ...scati, Boul. Montmartre 23; *Charvin*, Rue des Petits-Champs ...age de Choiseul; *Ragueneau*, Rue St. Honoré 202, opposite ...asins du Louvre; *Pâtisserie du Grand-Hôtel*, Place de l'Op... ...boust, Rue St. Honoré 163, Place du Théâtre-Français; *Rum*... ...r, Rue de Rivoli 226; *Bourbonneux*, Place du Havre 14; *G*... ...ue Victor-Hugo 4; *A la Dame Blanche*, Boul. St. Germain ... ... — The *Boulangeries-Pâtisseries* are less pretending: *Ladu*... *Royale* 16; *Cateloup*, Avenue de l'Opéra 25; *Wanner* (Vienne... ...e la Chaussée-d'Antin 3; *Rémy*, same street No. 45, etc. ...ntion also may be made of the *Petites Pâtisseries*, or stalls for ...cakes, buns, etc.; *e. g.* Boulevard St. Denis 13 ('*A Coupe-toujou*... ...the beginning of the Rue de la Lune, Boul. Bonne-Nouvelle. ...TERNOON TEA in the English style: *Afternoon Tea*, Place V... ...20; *Marlborough Tea Rooms*, Rue Cambon 5; *Colombin*, I... ...n 6; *British Dairy Company*, Rue Cambon 8; *Rumpelma*...

196   PARIS (IX°). — *Les Grands Cafés des Boulevards. — Une Terrasse.* — LL.

CAFÉ DE LA PAIX on Boulevard des Capucines. Compare to next page. As a young man in Paris in the 1960s, I sold *The New York Times* in front of this café. An American sitting at one of these tables, lonely as could be, invited me to join him for a drink just so he could speak English with someone. When I tried to order, the waiter told me, "I am sorry, we do not serve news vendors. You must leave." I folded my paper bag, placed it under the table and claimed that now my money was as good as anyone else's. This made no difference. He insisted. Furious, I walked inside to find the Maître d'. When this creep in a tuxedo confirmed what the first creep outside had said, I began raising my voice and gesticulating. Throwing glances left and right, this elegant gentleman quickly acquiesced and muttered impatiently, "Very well. This time, yes. But never again!"

196 PARIS. — Les Grands Cafés des Boulevards. — Une Terrasse. — LL.

CAFÉ DE LA PAIX on Boulevard des Capucines. Compare to previous page; same photographer, same shoot. Note differences: woman in white with large hat, two women behind her with striking hats. Others looking at camera in one and turned away in the other. Which photo was taken first?

BRASSERIE DE L'ESPÉRANCE, 19, place de la République, Paris. — E. AUDRAIN, Propriétaire

BRASSERIE DE L'ESPÉRANCE on Place de la République. Haussmann created Place de la République by erasing a large portion of the Grands Boulevards from the map. Lost were many old theaters that played to the working class population of the quarter. There was no pretense to the high brow here, and stage productions were full of sentimentality and blood-curdling screams. The uppermost balcony of these theaters with the cheapest seats was called Paradise, hence the film *The Children of Paradise*, a must for any Francophile.

BOULEVARD SAINT-DENIS. *Detail.*

Not a high quality photo but evocative neverthe-
less. To those imbued with a deep work ethic, casual
sitting around as seen here is borderline offensive.
A British observer of the period wrote of the café,
"People go to it to gossip and regale themselves, play
games, talk politics, read the newspapers, write letters, transact business, sit, think, dream, and rest
themselves. To the Anglo-Saxon the life that is led in
it seems a good deal like a walk about in a botanical
garden … a decidely artificial existence, but so long
as we must drink or be amused at all, we shall do
well to study the ways of the French." This facade has
been modernized and a clothing store now occupies
the site.

Vues de PARIS. — Le Boulevard Saint-Denis 17.

CAFÉ-RESTAURANT DE LA RÉGENCE, 161, Rue Saint-Honoré (Place du Théâtre-Français).
Intérieur du Café et de la Salle des Echecs.

CAFÉ-RESTAURANT DE LA RÉGENCE on Rue Saint-Honoré at the bottom of Avenue de l'Opéra. Every café had its clientele, be they artists, financiers, bankers, journalists, musicians, etc. At this café it was first-rate chess players. On any night as many as thirty boards were in play, with crowds hovering around tables to catch the action. On the wall hung a portrait of François-André Danican Philidor, the greatest chess player of the mid- to late-18TH century. On the left, a sign on the pillar reads "Symphony concert every evening from 9 PM to 1 AM."

Phot. S. Paris

CAFÉ AMÉRICAIN

Place de la République

GRANDE SALLE — BILLARDS

CAFÉ AMÉRICAIN. This is one of a series of postcards of this café, each of different rooms. Other Café Américains were on Boulevard des Capucines and Avenue de l'Opéra. This must have been a chain. Curious since America had no cafés of its own at that time.

6 — Maison des Chimères   Rue Saint-Antoine

RUE SAINT-ANTOINE. This café still stands in the Marais quarter. The wooden facade has been removed to reveal the original stonework. The 18TH century balcony with fantastical allegorical figures gives the café its present name, Café des Chimeres. This building and others on the street were slated for demolition in the 1940s in a grand project of urban renovation. Vigorous public protest forced the city to shelve the idea.

Postmarked 1961

Hi,

I don't site see—just sit & drink coffee and talk—en Francais! Look for the arrow and that's where you'll find me! Don't mean to sound fickle but forget what I said about everywhere else—Paris is THE place! How could I have wasted my time in hick towns like London, Oslo, Stockholm, Weisbaden, Copenhagen, Vienna or Rome? Have an attic room sur la rive gauche with chimney pots all over the horizon.   —Love, D.

BOULEVARD SAINT-GERMAIN. For years two of the most "in" Paris cafés have been the Café les Deux Magots (on right) and the Café de Flore (indicated by arrow). Strong allegiances develop and anyone who goes to one would never think of going to the other for all the obvious reasons, whatever they may be. The sender of the postcard on the next page preferred the Flore.

favorite camping spot near to my present place of residence...

*Major Luttenberg
155 Riverside Drive
New York City*

CAFÉ DE FLORE ON BOULEVARD SAINT-GERMAIN. At Rue Saint-Benoit.

*Postmarked 1938
Café de Flore—
favorite camping spot
near to my present place
of residence. This after-
noon I visited the Ile de
France at Havre—nice
but I'm glad to be back
at the "Flore" for my
after dinner coffee—
—Much love, Ruth*

Illustrated Paris

The invention of the postcard was a boon to artists who found a ready outlet for their talents. At first it was considered low class to illustrate for this questionable new mode of communication. But in a few years, as people became accustomed and the market grew, the art of the postcard flourished. Artists became highly sought after and careers were made.

September 22, 1908
Dear Susan Louise,

We have been receiving your letters plus the one mama wrote sending the clipping from the Chronicle. I hope she will send the papers as we are receiving no S.F. news. As I wrote I forgot to subscribe to the Chronicle. Has mama sent the rest of my pictures after giving aunt Marcella one. I have not received them yet. We are having beautiful fall weather.

—We all send love, Uncle Will

SAINT-GERMAIN-DES-PRÉS. This card was mailed from Cambridge, Massachusetts to San Francisco and demonstrates how at the height of their popularity postcards were often bought abroad for future use in America, knowing that they would be a treat on the receiving end. Given the hardships in the world of newspaper publishing today, the request for the *San Francisco Chronicle* is particularly interesting.

May 15, 1907
This is our second night
here—Our trip is fine.
Love, Florence and Jack

THE LOUVRE. Florence and Jack are not used to the divided back post-card. Like other Americans in France, they have written the address in the right place, but leaves the message area empty and writes on the side of the illustration. The divided back was introduced in France in 1904 and in the U.S. in 1907. Perhaps not before she left home.

TOUR SAINT-JACQUES.   **PLACE DE LA RÉPUBLIQUE.**

NOTRE-DAME.

RUE MOUFFETARD.

Paris   St Germain des Prés.

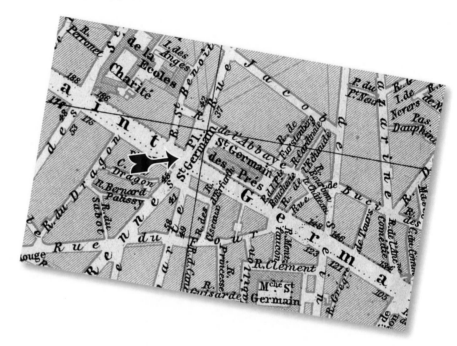

CHURCH OF SAINT-GERMAIN-DES-PRÉS.

Les Halles.– S.ᵗ Eustache.

Ici l'on vend des fleurs, des choux et des poissons,
On y vend des navets, du bétail, des melons.–
Mais on offre à l'église – ô charité divine !–
Le céleste banquet à l'homme qui chemine.......

Pierre Weyrat

LES HALLES. Church of Saint-Eustache. The first stone was laid in 1532.

Arc de Triomphe de l'Etoile.

Souvenir de la Belle Jardinière
2, Rue du Pont-Neuf. PARIS.

ARC DE TRIOMPHE.

SERIE 535. N° 23

BOULEVARD DES CAPUCINES.

PARIS

A scene from Paris for our Geneve.

Mamma & Papa.

BOULEVARD DES CAPUCINES.

PÉTROLE HAHN

LE TRÉSOR DES CHEVEUX

PARIS. Une Entrée du Parc Monceau.

LOIR LUIGI

PARC MONCEAU.

(98)

Les Halles

Les Halles had been located at the same spot on the Right Bank for hundreds of years when the Paris City Council decided in 1963 to move the market out of the city, to the suburb of Rungis. The question then was what to do with the 19TH century steel-and-glass pavilions designed by Victor Baltard and universally recognized as a gem of French architecture. The decision to tear them down met stiff protest from the public, but to no avail.

American Orrin Hein made an offer to buy all the pavilions and transport them back to America. "Impossible; too much breakage," he was told by the Prefect of Paris. Dubbed "Superman" by the Paris media, Hein managed to pressure President Pompidou into saving two of the pavilions. One stands in the suburb of Nogent-sur-Marne, the other in Yokohama, Japan. The rebuilt Les Halles turned out to be a grand catastrophe of urban planning—a case study in how to kill a once thriving neighborhood.

In 2002, Mayor Delanoe began a long process to tear down and rebuild Les Halles. A competition was held, four finalists were chosen, and in 2004 the project was awarded to French architect David Mangin. Projects of this scale are enormously complex and take decades to carry out. To date nothing has changed.

62 — C. PARIS. — Les Halles Centrales Collections ND. Phot.

RUE BALTARD. In Les Halles, the Paris central markets. In the distance, the 16TH century church of Saint-Eustache.

540. – PARIS

Le Carreau des Halles
Légumes et Salades

LES HALLES, the central markets. Green grocer section.

PARIS. Les Halles Centrales
Pavillon de la Marée

LES HALLES. Seafood section.

399. PARIS – *Un coin des Halles le matin* C. M.

LES HALLES. On the left, Rue Baltard. Right, Rue Berger.

192 PARIS. — Les Halles à 6 heures du matin. — LL.

LES HALLES. Rue Rambuteau. In the distance, the church of Saint Eustache. This street was created in the 1830s by the Prefect of the same name. At its creation this was one of the widest streets in Paris. During the makeover of Les Halles in the 1970s, most of the buildings on the right were torn down and this street was made narrow once again.

TOUT PARIS

SPEC.^{te} DE VIN BLANC DE CHABLIS

COLLECTION F. FLEURY.

1234 — Les Halles le matin - Rue Buger (Ier arr^t)

LES HALLES, morning. Rue Berger looking west from Rue de la Lingerie. The first two buildings were constructed by Haussmann in the 1860s. In fine condition and with years of life before them, they were demolished in the 1970s during the modern makeover of Les Halles. In their place stands a hotel in the style of generic modernism.

459. PARIS Les Halles   C. M.

LES HALLES, the central markets. Rue Berger.

Paris in Detail

The average postcard gets only a casual glance. But deep seeing, entering into the detail of the image, brings it to life and allows one to penetrate into the world of the photo. It was only after looking at these postcards closely under a magnifying glass, in the days before Photoshop, that their richness was revealed to me. Some postcards at first looked like doubles of cards I already had but turned out to be different photos taken only minutes apart by the same photographer on the same shoot. Others revealed clever manipulation of the image by adding vehicles to make an old card look new. Other cards revealed compelling expressions and interactions between people, while others were simply surprising. Who would expect to look at a Paris postcard close-up and find Buffalo Bill?

966 — PARIS. Le Pont des Arts et l'Institut. ND Phot.

A woman shields her face from the photographer perched high on a ladder.

PONT DES ARTS. The first metallic footbridge built across the Seine in 1803. Opening day drew tens of thousands of people. Until 1848, all pedestrians paid one sou to cross. In 1851 the bridge was shortened by one arch when the Quai de Conti on the Left Bank side was widened. In 1979 a barge struck a pier, causing extensive damage. The bridge was closed for several years and entirely rebuilt, shortened again by one arch.

AVENUE DE L'OPÉRA.

Detail of page 132. A fashionable woman strolls down the avenue. A man parked at the curb takes a break from pedaling his cart. The lettering on the front tells us that he is a vendor of fine cheese. An expensive automobile with a well dressed driver trundles along.

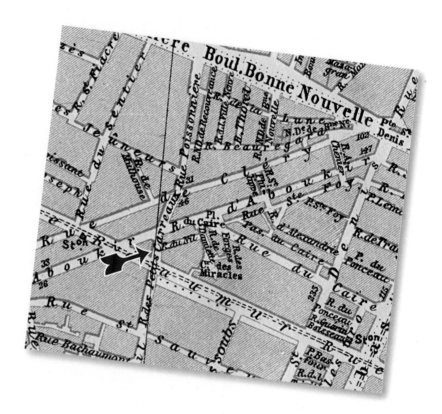

RUE DU NIL. *Actual size.* The sign overhead reads "Here is Erneste's Palace, a.k.a. The Savior." A second floor sign reads "Annual sales, 50,000 pairs of shoes!" Rue du Nil is one of the smallest streets in Paris. It took on the name of Africa's River Nile in 1867 to commemorate Napoleon's campaign in Egypt. Two other nearby streets, Rues du Caire and Rue Damiette, did the same.

RUE DU NIL. *Detail.* An astonishing group, each person with a clear and distinct personality. Typically, Erneste with an "E" at the end would be a woman's name. But this is the exception to the rule. Back then Erneste with an "E" could be either a man's or a woman's name. Which one is Erneste? A note in pencil on the back of this card reveals this much: "Ernest Bresson Chausurres, 1 rue du Nil." So Ernest is a man. But which one?

872. PARIS — Carrefour des Feuillantines E. L. D.

RUE DES FEUILLANTINES. *Actual size.* It is impossible to walk around central Paris and not pass through thick layers of history. Émile Zola lived on this street. A giant of 19TH century French literature, he authored of one of the most renowned pieces of journalism ever written: "J'accuse," a piece excoriating the French government for its anti-Semitism in its handling of the infamous Dreyfus affair. Victor Hugo spent his youth in a house at number 8. George Sand lived at number 97.

July 29, 1907
Ma Chere! Parlee vous Francé?
Oui-Oui! Madamoiselle.
—Y.K.W.

RUE DES FEUILLANTINES. *Detail.*

Drove by here this evening E.K.S. July 21.

30. – PARIS. – Le Grand Palais aux Champs-Elysées

GRAND PALAIS. *Actual size.* The largest iron and glass structure in the world, built for the World's Fair of 1900. Closed in 1993 because of deterioration, it was reopened in 2005 after extensive restoration. Note, lines of glue were laid down on the card and sparkle was applied.

GRAND PALAIS. *Details of previous page. Image on left:* A woman bends down to pick up her umbrella. Lines of glue were laid down on the card and sparkle was then applied. *Image on right:* Three exhausted sandwich men nap on a bench. Their signs advertise a puppet show, Grand Guignol, with Docteur Goudron (Tar) and Professeur Plume (Feather).

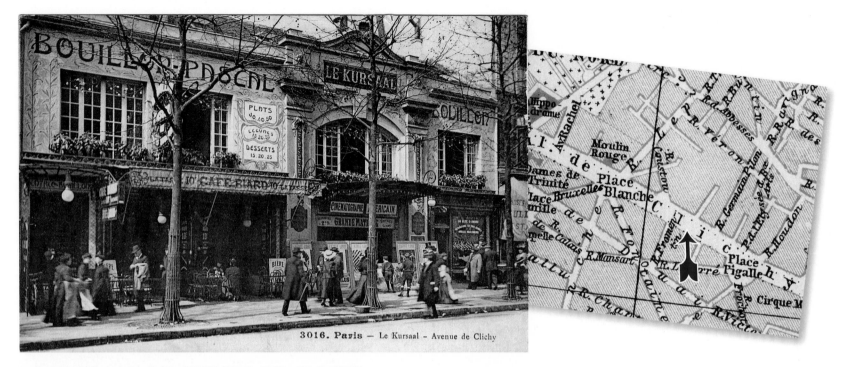

3016. Paris — Le Kursaal - Avenue de Clichy

LE KURSAAL ON AVENUE DE CLICHY. *Actual size.* On the left is a working class restaurant "Bouillon Pascal." The sign "Le Kursaal" is a cinema. A note on the other side of the card says "Founded 1906, disappeared," but does that refer to the restaurant or the cinema? Compare with next page.

LE KURSAAL. *Detail.* The sign over the entry into the Kursaal reads "Cinematographe Americain." It is the early 1900s and American films are already playing in Paris. Another sign says, "Big Matinee. Shows at 2:30 P.M." Two men and two boys gaze at the posters standing in front. A board across the entry shows that the cinema is not yet open.

1278 PARIS (IIᵉ). — *Rue Saint-Denis prise de la Rue Réaumur.* — LI.

RUE SAINT-DENIS looking north. *Actual size.* For centuries
this was one of the main thoroughfares cutting north-south through Paris.
In the distance, Porte Saint-Denis. See next page.

RUE SAINT-DENIS. *Detail of previous page.* Note boys on left. On right, a young girl walks towards camera. Oh that waist! A man in the distance looks at photographer on ladder. Bouillon Chartier, on left, is a famous working-class eatery, located today on Rue du Faubourg Montmartre and catering largely to tourists.

1178. PARIS – Rue de la Huchette   C. M.

RUE DE LA HUCHETTE. *Actual size.* During the Middle Ages this street was a footpath through a vineyard. Today it is thoroughly touristed up with swarming crowds day and night, a far cry from the quiet street in this photo. Parisians rarely come here. Note how the street is wide and becomes narrow. This is because the first buildings on left and right were built by Haussmann. His plan was to continue this to the end—one of many projects never carried out. Off to the right is Rue de la Harpe.

CARTE POSTALE

La Correspondance au recto n'est pas acceptée par tous les pays étrangers
(Se renseigner à la Poste)

Côté correspondance.   Côté adresse:

Dear Edgar, July 27/190

Mr Edgar A.
8 surf ave
Ocean Grove
N. J.

U. S. A.

July 27, 1907

My Dear Edgar;

How could you forget your mother as never to write a line? I think of you all the time. I hope I am mistaken and that your letters have failed to reach me.

—Lovingly, Mother

RUE DE LA HUCHETTE. *Detail.* Is the young woman reading a newspaper or perhaps crocheting? A postman is approaching in the distance. Note the curious curtains hanging on the doorway up the street.

GATE TO BOIS DE BOULOGNE. *Detail.* The hand tinting is obvious.

May 31, 1905
The city is looking its best
for the boy king but it is not the
Paris I remember. It is more like
London, smoky & dirty & the
atmosphere full of the smell of
gasoline from the automobile.

BOIS DE BOULOGNE, ALLÉE DES ACACIAS. *Detail.* Mrs. Swann of Marcel Proust fame walked along here nearly every day. Note right hand drive auto coming down the road.

September 2, 1913
My Dear Little Mama,
   I am here in fine style. This is by far the most beautiful city I have ever seen. It is beyond description. I am in love with it. I am so sorry you are having such trouble with the McDougals. Just let the lawyers go on with the proceedings. I think it will pay, so does pop. I wish I was there to help you. Tell the lawyer about the gas stove.
   —Richard

BOULEVARD DES CAPUCINES from Place de l'Opéra. *Detail.* On the right, Café de la Paix. On the left, a man tries to hail a taxi.

98 PARIS. — L'Hôtel de Cluny construit en 1490 par l'Abbé Jacques d'Amboise. — LL.

MUSÉE CLUNY. *Actual size.* One of the few medieval buildings still standing in Paris, today a museum for art of the Middle Ages. During the Revolution, insurgents cut the heads off statues on the facade of Notre-Dame thinking they were the Kings of France. In reality they were saints. In the 1970s a building on the Right Bank sprang a leak in the basement. Workers digging up the floor came upon these heads, buried for over two hundred years and, it is said, all facing in the direction of the cathedral. These originals today are in this museum. At actual size one easily misses the detail and the fine hand tinting of this postcard.

Detail. Note the fifteen people in this photo and the finesse and variety of their coloring, as well as that of the flowers in the foreground.

Detail. Four women,
two prams, one child.

857. PARIS - Rue Saint-Dominique
(Angle Avenue de la Bourdonnais)   E.L.D.

RUE SAINT-DOMINIQUE from the Avenue de la Bourdonnais. This was not a postcard for the typical tourist unless they happened to be staying on this street. But one detail might be of interest, particularly for the passing American. See next page.

RUE SAINT-DOMINIQUE. From the Avenue de la Bourdonnais. *Detail.* Buffalo Bill was in Paris with his rodeo and this was his publicity office. His first appearance in Paris in 1883 created a sensation. Nothing could be more exotic to the French than cowboys and Indans from the wild west. He returned in 1889 for the World's Fair, but attendance was compromised because of a cab strike. Among his lineup of attractions that year was famed female sharpshooter Annie Oakley. The sign on this storefront dates the card. "Buffalo Bill's Wild West and Congress of Rough Riders of the World" is a name he took in 1893. This is therefore from his appearance in 1905.

162, PARIS — Les Grands Cafés des Boulevards - A. P.   Public Housse of

CAFÉ DE LA PAIX. *Actual size.* Compare to next page. At first glance,
the same postcard. Detail shows otherwise.

343 PARIS. — Le Café de la Paix. — LL.

CAFÉ DE LA PAIX. *Actual size.* Same day, same photographer as previous page.

1915   PARIS (Ier et IIe). — L'Avenue de l'Opéra et l'Académie Nationale de Mu...

AVENUE DE L'OPERA. *Actual size.* Compare to next page. Both views were taken on the same shoot. Also see page 109.

Detail. Man watches photographer.

May 18, 1914

    Paris is lovely. Fashions extreme. Susanne lovely, you must part your hair on the side, screw the rest tight to your head, wear very small hat over right eye—skirt short to ankle very tight, overskirt almost as long but very full— to be in it. Have seen wonderful sights but U. S. is good enough for me to live in.   —*Love to all, Florence*

Detail. Compare to previous page. Behind the woman crossing the street we see the same man watching the photographer.

1915   PARIS (Ier et IIe). — L'Avenue de l'Opera et l'Académie Nationale de Musique (Théâtre de l'Opéra). — LL.

AVENUE DE L'OPÉRA. *Actual size.*

PARIS --- Boulevard Saint-Michel

A . B.

BOULEVARD SAINT-MICHEL looking north, one block from the Seine. Compare to next page. Same photographer, same day, same shoot.

PARIS — Boulevard Saint-Michel

A. B.

BOULEVARD SAINT-MICHEL looking north, one block from the Seine. See detail on next page. Both cards postmarked 1912.

BOULEVARD SAINT-MICHEL. *Detail of previous page.* A barber shop on the left (COIFFEUR) shows the popularity of postcards with racks on display. Among them is the Mona Lisa. Note woman in window above COIFFEUR sign looking at photographer. Note the sign down the street for Boulangerie, Patisserie St. Michel. Compare to next page.

BAKERY, PASTRY SHOP at 10 Boulevard Saint-Michel. Compare to previous page.

RUE SAINT-ANTOINE looking west. Food vendors line the curb. Note man in foreground looking in his coin purse. In the distance, a man in a white shirt on a ladder. Compare to next page.

RUE SAINT-ANTOINE looking west. Compare to previous page. Man with coin purse now talks with the vendor. Man in the distance is lower on the ladder. Is he going up or down? Which photo was shot first?

888. PARIS
Rue Mouffetard
E. L. D.

RUE MOUFFETARD. Two cards taken by the same photographer, same shoot. Note little boys on bottom right shielding their eyes from the sun. Horse and cart are in same place in both. The card on left is of higher quality.

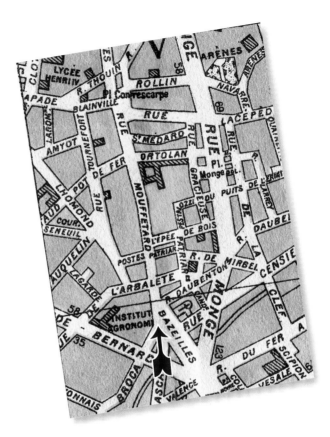

RUE MOUFFETARD. Compare to previous page. Charles Garnier, architect of the opera house that bears his name, was born in this street in 1824.

RUE DE SEINE looking north. *Actual size*. Cross street is Rue de Buci. On the left a woman appears to be helping another at the curb, while a woman at the corner looks on with concern.

Disappeared Paris

*T*he value of the postcard as a witness to the city in transformation is only revealed through time. Photographers shooting views for postcards could not have known what dimension their work would take on as the city continued to evolve. Most of the photographs in this book show us streets and buildings that are still in place, yet we can't help but notice what has been lost in these pictures: a city that was quieter, slower, not as dense, some would say a more civil city. But it is the views of sites that have been wiped from the map that shake us the most. This is when the simple 10 cent postcard becomes a monument to loss and brings us face to face with questions of progress and conservation. Was the trade-off worth it? What have we gained, what have we lost?

CONVENT OF THE ABBAYE AUX BOIS. Built in 1640, this convent was nationalized during the Revolution along with all other ecclesiastical property in France. By 1819 the pendulum had swung back and the site was once again in the hands of a religious order. The entrance stood at 16 Rue de Sevres near the Bon Marché department store. Madame Recamier, immortalized in the painting of Jacques-Louis David, lived here from 1819 to 1849. Her famed literary salon was much frequented by her friend Chateaubriand, the father of French Romanticism. What was spared by the Revolution was lost to the needs of modernity. The abbey was torn down in 1906 for the opening of Boulevard Raspail.

Cheval Blanc. Sous Louis XIV, départ des c

RUE MAZET. AUBERGE DU CHEVAL BLANC. The White Horse Inn. Dates from the 17TH century. This was a stagecoach inn serving Orleans, Tours and Bordeaux. The young boys on the left stand in front of a poster advertising that new attraction in Paris, the Eiffel Tower. The inn was demolished in the early 1890s. The present building dates from the 1990s and is a student restaurant.

56.- Auberge du Cheval Blanc. Sous Louis XIV, départ des carrosses pour Orléans
5, rue Mazet
Vieux Paris B. C. (déposé)

RUE SAINT-JULIEN LE PAUVRE seen from Rue Galande towards Rue de la Bucherie. The building at the end of the street in the card on left is an annex to the Paris hospital, Hotel Dieu. Note the tower of Notre-Dame behind. The card on the right was taken after the annex had been torn down in 1908. Behind the wall on the right was a scrubby yard with another wing of the annex, also torn down. Today this space is a gem of a small park called Square Viviani. Compare these postcards to next page.

(146)

175. — *Paris.* – Vieil Hôtel-Dieu.

RUE DE LA BUCHERIE from Rue Lagrange. The river Seine is on the immediate right. Large building is same as at end of Rue Saint-Julien le Pauvre on previous page. The walkway extends across Rue de la Bucherie to another wing of the hospital annex, also demolished in 1908. This portion of the Rue de la Bucherie was eliminated when Square Viviani was established in 1928.

619. PARIS - Entrée de la Cour du Dragon, Rue de Rennes
C.L.C.

COUR DU DRAGON on Rue de Rennes. Built in 1732. Designed by Pierre de Vigny, architect of the handsome building at 42 Rue Francois-Miron in the Marais. Survived Haussmann's rebuilding of Paris only to be brought down by a later generation of barbarians. The courtyard was torn down in 1926, the facade in 1958. A Monoprix department store was built on the spot. The winged dragon over the entry was saved and is on display in the Louvre. Compare to next page.

COUR DU DRAGON. *Detail.* This passageway was a small center of ironmongers manufacturing wrought iron gates, balconies, and other ironworks. About one hundred families lived in the floors above. An exit at the end gave onto Rue du Dragon.

304. — *Paris.* - Cour du Dragon.

RUE DU PRE SAINT-GERVAIS. During the postcard craze every street, no matter how humble, had its moment of glory in print. These neighborhoods in the east of Paris rarely saw a tourist yet were integral to the rest of Paris in their "feel." Away from the bustling center you still felt like you were in Paris. To close your eyes and magically reappear on this street today would be a shock to anyone's sensibility. A banal modernism has swept through it and Paris no longer lives here.

TOUT PARIS

1803 - La Rue de Belleville (XIX° et XX° arr¹)
à la hauteur de la rue Compans

COLLECTION F. FLEURY.

RUE DE BELLEVILLE. Rue de Compans on the right. A short distance from the photo on previous page. On a contemporary map of Paris we find these streets in the same place, but nothing seen here stands.

687 bis **TOUT PARIS** — Rue Vilin (XXᵉ arrᵗ)

RUE VILIN. Writer Georges Perec was born in this street in 1936. His best known work, *La Vie mode d'emploi* (*Life: A User's Manual*) won the Prix Médicis in 1978. Nothing remains of this street or its buildings. In its place stands a brutal 20TH century. Anyone wishing to see this street today need only go to Google Maps and enter Rue Vilin. Handkerchiefs are recommended.

1244. PARIS – Palais-Royal – Galerie d'Orléans

GALERIE D'ORLEANS. Located on the south side of the Palais Royal garden, it was on this spot that the first arcade, or covered passageway, was built in Paris in 1786. Known as the Galerie de Bois, it stood until 1827. This arcade was built in its place in 1829. The success of the Galerie de Bois sparked the grand vogue of covered passageways throughout Paris and the rest of Europe. The invention of the department store in the 1850s emptied these once fashionable consumer havens. Desolate and forlorn, many were destroyed. This one was torn down in 1936. Today one finds a large open space here. All that remains are the two columns at the very end.

12 — Rue de Venise (XIV siècle) à droite, cabaret de l'Epée de
fréquenté par Molière Racine, Marivaux etc. et première académie nationale d

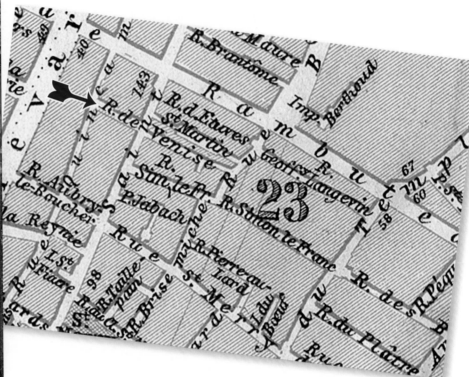

RUE DE VENISE. Only a small unrecognizable portion of this street remains. Most of the neighborhood was torn down in the 1930s after being tagged a slum. Nothing was rebuilt in its place until the Centre George Pompidou in the 1970s. Note the panels mounted on the windows, not uncommon in old photos of Paris. They are a mystery, even for Parisians. Theories about their function abound but are all hypothetical. Note woman looking from window.

RUE BRISEMICHE. *Detail.* This street was created in 1420 as part of the cloister of the Eglise Saint-Merri, a short walk from here. Its name derives from a bakery that stood here that made bread for the canons of the church. Everything here was demolished in the 1930s in a program of slum clearance. The Pompidou Center is only steps away. Note panels on windows.

71. — Cour de l'auberge du Compas d'Or, commencement XVIᵉ siècle
Hangar qui abrita jadis les coches partant pour Dreux
64, rue Montorgueil

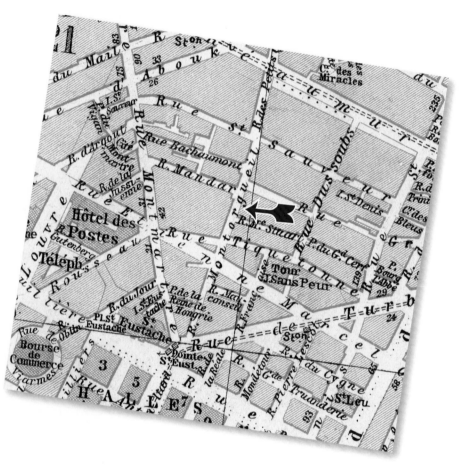

64 RUE MONTORGUEIL. Courtyard of the Auberge du Compas d'Or, Golden Compass Inn. Wooden hangar dates from 16TH century. Stage-coaches for the inn were kept in this courtyard. Demolished in 1914.

72 RUE MONTORGUEIL. Hotel du Compas d'Or, Golden Compass Inn. Dates from the 16TH century and was a stagecoach inn for travelers to and from Normandy. The building was torn down in 1914. A few doors down at number 66 lived the notorious Pierre François Lacenaire This gentleman, poet and murderer was the inspiration for Dosteovsky's *Crime and Punishment*. He is also portrayed in the film *The Children of Paradise*. In 1836, on the morning of his execution, Lacenaire smoked a cigar and drank a glass of cognac. On the scaffold the blade of the guillotine fell and stopped inches short of his neck. The damp weather had swollen the grooves and the blade did not fall all the way. A second attempt was successful.

27. — Entrée de l'hotel du Compas d'Or
72, rue Montorgueil

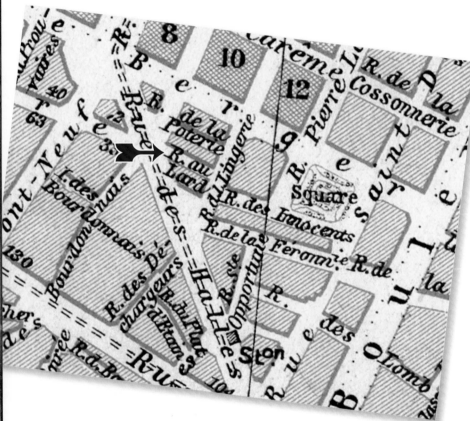

RUE AU LARD. This street in the Les Halles quarter dates from the 16TH century. The name derives from butcher shops that were installed here. Everything was torn down in the 1970s. A modern hotel stands on this spot today. Note man peeking around corner on left side of arch.

NEW YORK HERALD, European Edition, located at 49 Avenue de l'Opéra. Today's technology can deliver news to us anywhere in the world through our laptop and keep us in touch with loved one at all hours of the day and night via email and cell phone. Consequently something people have known for centuries has been erased from the bandwidth of human experience—homesickness. The feeling of going to the poste restante or American Express office longing for a letter from home and finding nothing was its own kind of heartsickness. Having two or three letters dropped in one's hand was an unparalleled joy made only better by reading and rereading them throughout the day. Newspapers were a vital link to keeping in touch. The *Herald* had a reading room with as many as 500 newspapers where Americans abroad found momentary respite from a feeling no young person today will ever know.

Restaurant de nuit à Montmartre — A night restaurant in Montmartre

Paris by Night

*T*he legendary night life of Paris at the turn of the 20TH century was centered around Montmartre on the Boulevards Clichy, Rochechourt, Place Blanche, and Place Pigalle. There is a reason for this location. In the late 1780s, Paris was encircled by a massive wall, the Fermiers Généraux, that ran along where these boulevards stand today. With over fifty ports of entry into the city, this wall was not a fortification but rather had been erected to enforce a complicated system of taxation on goods brought into Paris, e.g., alcohol, foodstuffs, wood, etc. Because wine was cheaper outside of Paris, drinking establishments, cabarets and dance halls set up just outside the wall. When Haussmann enlarged Paris in 1860 and the tax wall came down, the city continued to grow on the footprint of Paris nightlife that had already been established. For years Montmartre and Pigalle were synonymous with everything that made the hair on any mother's head stand on end.

54. PARIS — Le Moulin Rouge C. M.

THE MOULIN ROUGE

opened its doors in 1889 and was an immediate sensation. Creators Charles Zidler and Joseph Oller were master showmen who knew what it took to captivate the public. They chose a spot in the red-light district, and provided racy entertainment and a well crafted interior to create an atmosphere of euphoria and other-worldiness unlike anything anyone had seen. In the buttoned-down world of the late 19TH century, can-can girls kicking high were guaranteed success. Toulouse-Lautrec was a regular. The windmill is a facsimile.

January 27, 1913
I wish we could
have one Saturday
night together here.
—Frank

*This is the naughty
Moulin Rouge—Red Mill.
I've never been there.*

POST CARD Carte
BRIEFKAA
CARTOLINA POSTALE – OT
This is the
naughty Moul
Rouge – Red
Mill. I've nev
been there.

PARIS. — LE MOULIN ROUGE (PLACE BLANCHE).

Will tell you about this restaurant when I come home. Don't let me forget it.

143. PARIS - Le Moulin Rouge

LES MIRLITONS

Will tell you about this restaurant when I come home. Don't let me forget it.

Back of card: *We have seen many places of interest today spending much of the time in a motor car with a guide. We readily understand now why every one loves Paris—I should love sometime to spend a year here.*

—Sara

*Bringing your wife to Paris is like bringing
your own meal to a banquet.*

—*Max Rafelson*
(of Louis Graner Co.)

143. PARIS (18e) — Le Moulin Rouge

Mlle. Bertha Bandell
New York City
Etats Unis d'Amérique
185 E. 115 St.

May 25, 19—
    Here is the place I formerly
went to church every night
avant le guerre.
                    —John

52 M. PARIS — Vue Générale du Moulin Rouge (XVIII° arr¹)

MOULIN ROUGE ON PLACE BLANCHE. From this vantage point one sees the original music hall arranged on a garden. Years later as the club grew everything was enclosed. The picturesque constructions on the left and right with the turret and gabled roof were lost. Compare to next page.

1287 — PARIS. Boulevard de Clichy, le Ciel et l'Enfer. ND Phot.

TWIN CABARETS ON BOULEVARD CLICHY. Heaven on the left, Hell on the right. Torn down in the 1960s.

August 23, 1913

 Helas! Quelques jours encore est cette vie de Paris ne sera plus qu'un beau reve.

 (Alas! Only a few more days and this Paris life will be no more than a dream.)

—*H. Armand*

1561 PARIS — « L'Enfer » Boulevard de Clichy. — LL.

PARIS — Le Cabaret du « Lapin Agile »
Rue des Saules   E. L. D.

CABARET LAPIN AGILE, famous for its associations with Picasso, Utrillo, etc., it was well known in its own day as a haunt for artists, writers, and eccentrics of all types. Here on the *butte*, the hill, in a rural setting when Montmartre was still a village, one felt far away, a happy repair for those who wanted the draw of the grand city but could not afford its expensive cafés and restaurants.

140. – PARIS (Montmartre). — La Rue Saint-Vincent. - Cabaret du "Lapin Agile".

CABARET LAPIN AGILE. Rue des Saules on left. Straight ahead, Rue Saint Vincent. Note water carrier.

692. PARIS — Le Cabaret des Truands - Boulevard de Clichy

1566 PARIS (XVIIIᵉ). — Le Cabaret des Truands

CABARET DES TRUANDS. Boulevard de Clichy. Note the remodel.

CABARET DES TRUANDS.

Boulevard de Clichy. *Detail*. This spot at 100 Boulevard de Clichy was home to a string of cabarets including this one from 1914–1918. None lasted long. In 1922 the cabaret Les Deux Anes opened and is still running today. Boulevard de Clichy has seen its share of notables. Degas lived at number 6 and died there in 1917. Picasso lived at number 9 in 1909. Daumier lived at number 36. A few doors down is the Moulin Rouge.

319. ~ PARIS. ~ L'Hippodrome

HIPPODROME ON BOULEVARD DE CLICHY. Built with almost 6,000 places for the 1900 World's Fair. An American observer attending the fair spent an evening at the Hippodrome and wrote, "This is one of the great sights of modern Paris, the most enormous assembly room that I ever saw. Everything was perfect, even the indecency, of which there was the usual French proportion ... the French people, with all their refinement have little real modesty or delicacy. I never saw anything so laughably shameless as some of the performances were ... these were specimens of superlative acrobatics, equestrianism, etc... I did think of Rome in the ages of rottenness and decay." The site had difficulty after the fair. It became a skating rink, an orchestra hall, a sports arena, and finally the world's largest movie theatre. The Boston Symphony played there in 1917. It was torn down around 1974.

1572 PARIS (XVIIIe). — L'Élysée-Montmartre. — LL.

ELYSÉE MONTMARTRE, a popular dance hall at 44 Boulevard de Rouchechouart. Street uphill is Rue Steinkerque. The building is still in place, although somewhat tattered.

It is impossible to discuss Paris postcards of the early 20TH century and not at least mention the risqué cards that gave Paris its racy reputation. The earliest of these postcards featured young girls striking artistic poses in full body stockings as seen on the right. A shock to Victorian modesty, for sure. In the aftermath of World War I, the Roaring Twenties brought a new freedom, or as some said, a new licentiousness. Partial nudes such as the young girl above would have been unthinkable ten years earlier. These cards were typical of the period. This model posed for dozens of such cards. She was not the most striking of beauties but the camera certainly loved her.

Appendix

❖

*L*ouis Wolowski, the man who single-handedly led the effort to introduce the postcard in France, wrote the following article in January 1873, weeks before the first cards were issued, laying out the potential of this new mode of communication. It took him over a year of sustained effort, knowing when to move and when to hold back, to achieve what almost every other country in Europe had already understood.

This fascinating document, a brilliant and reasoned exposition around something so utterly common today, is worth reading in full. The translation is mine.

❖

THE POSTCARD IN DIFFERENT COUNTRIES

After studying the latest report from the English Postmaster General I said it would not be long before France adopts the *postcard* that has been so successful on the other side of the Channel.

The law of December 20, 1872 has realized this wish: it now fully applies this new means of communication that allows for the rapid transmission of thought and becomes a fecund instrument in multiplying relationships in both the family and commerce.

In order to fully grasp the progress we have made we must first understand the nature of this agent and the results it has already demonstrated.

The *carte postale*, which will fulfill in France what the *postcard* does in England, or the *carte-correspondence* in Germany, Austria, Switzerland and Belgium, etc, is an uncovered letter sent by means of a card approximately 12 by 8 centimeters. On one side is a pre-affixed stamp with a space clearly delineated for the name and address at the point of destination. The other side is blank and is to receive the communication that one desires to transmit, be it a handwritten message or a printed advertisement.

One obtains a postcard with the stamp already affixed at a rate officially determined by the Post Office, and one can use them as often as one wishes by simply throwing them into a mailbox.

Postcards allow one to save money. The postal rate is usually half the letter rate and one can forego the expense of purchasing writing paper, an envelope, or the means of closing the envelope. But this in itself does not describe all the advantages of the postcard. One must also take into account the time saving aspect realized in so many ways.

Indeed, when one wants to transmit a thought or desire one will have at one's disposition a complete instrument that does away with looking for a sheet of paper, an envelope, wax, or a stamp and which allows one to write on the fly, wherever one may be, and with whatever instrument one may have at one's disposal, e.g., pen or pencil.

One can do away with the banal formalities of politeness that make ordinary letters unnecessarily long, and one becomes accustomed to messages that are clear and concise.

The postcard should have been born in England where the cost of time is so well known, "le temps c'est l'argent, time is money" and where this dictum is so well practiced. Saving time we become richer, not only in the domain of industry but in the realm of ordinary affairs. We pleasantly stretch out our lives as we become more efficient in the workplace and reduce lost time.

The postcard is in perfect synch with this tendency towards efficiency. It allows us to bring together a savings on the material plane with a savings no less worthwhile in the realm of human existence.

We should not think that the postcard, in doing away with the traditional formalities of correspondence, in any way harms or diminishes the more delicate sentiments that bring charm to one's life. Real politesse does not need a vocabulary made up of the most common compliments. As for the more tender relations in a family, these can find expression in brief phrases that provide satisfaction to those suffering the ennui of separation.

The electric telegraph has realized a wonderful progress in this regard. In a certain respect it has eliminated distance and in the most grave circumstances allows for instant communication that calms the anguish brought on by separation. For nations as well as individuals it brings people together in their feelings and relationships creating a kind of community for those separated by distance.

More modestly, by the way in which it promotes relationships and saves time and money, the postcard provides a similar service. It serves as a commodious vehicle of communication between families and commercial interests in cases where there is no need to conceal a message's contents. The rapidity of transmission is made easy by an instrument always available whether one is simply away from home or on a long voyage.

Carrying a small supply of postcards, one is never caught short when the need suddenly arises to send a message for whatever reason. We find this confirmed in countries where the postcard functions at the same rate as a normal letter and has integrated itself so successfully because of its numerous intrinsic advantages.

To be sure, the postcard does not pretend to replace the closed letter nor to eliminate the need to communicate intimate thoughts. It simply serves as a useful adjunct to relationships that have no need for extrapolation or any kind of mystery. Rather than reducing the number of ordinary letters, the postcard's ease of use multiplies communication and increases their number. This will be made evident as we examine the results of the postcard in countries such as England, Germany, Switzerland and Belgium.

The wonderful invention of photography lead many to believe that artists would have nothing more to do when in truth they have never been busier. Photography, with all its mechanics, has to the contrary, created an ever greater desire to contemplate the likeness of our loved ones due to the genius and soul of the real artist, the painter or sculptor … Daguerre takes nothing away from Ingres, Scheffer, Delaroche or Flandrin.

The missive of the postcard will take its place next to the letter fulfilling a need to transmit other thoughts than those of a letter. The charm and the efficiency of our epistolary relationships loses nothing. The promptness and brevity of the first experiments will lead to longer missives of a different nature. The lowering of the cost increases the mass of the product and thus helps increase consummation. This truth of the commercial world is applied in all realms.

And we must not underestimate how the more concise form of message transmitted by the postcard will influence the style of writing by increasing the clarity in how we express our thoughts. If a Sévigné were to come into the world today the postcard would not stop her from charming us.

One accusation made against the postcard stands out. In the old days there was a style of writing that passed information onto future generations in a brief form with great vitality. Today when there are so many more useful ways to spend our time we use a brief and concise, might I even say a more severe language to instantly transmit our sentiments and thoughts over great distances.

It is not without reason that we bring up these considerations that explain how the postcard functions, its usefulness, and the service it renders. As we penetrate further into the nature of this innovation we will better understand the many forms it takes on and will fear less what has for so long been a reason for rejecting the postcard: that it will reduce postal revenues.

It is not necessary to point out that this should be a secondary consideration given that the post office is above all a public service with so many advantages to the public that the issue of revenue should be moot.

Given the painful circumstances that we currently experience (Franco-Prussian war, The Commune) while there are certain fundamental truths that are less applied, the future will compensate us beyond the sacrifice we are presently forced to endure.

Of course we must be constantly aware of any potential loss of revenue as well as trends that can increase the Treasury's revenue. Being legitimately careful in this regard, we must also be careful not to sacrifice for some momentary concern an actual source of revenue. That would be like cutting down the tree to harvest the fruit.

Without falling into meaningless arguments, and so as to remain within the framework of the question we are examining here, we can reassure those who fear the postcard as a danger to public revenue.

It must be said that the excessive increase in postal rates in France is far from having increased postal revenue and has, to the contrary, reduced the amount of items sent through the mail which is a real calamity. While in other countries the rate of correspondence in all categories has steadily increased and this provides great social benefit.

The high cost of postage for ordinary letters by necessity brings about a relatively high rate for the postcard—that being 10 centimes within the circumscription of a single post office and 15 centimes for the rest of the country. This is far too expensive. But we are still in a stage of experimentation, and one can only hope that in lowering the rate of an ordinary letter to 10 and 20 centimes, we can also reduce the postcard rate to 5 and 10

centimes. As we wait for this eventuality the postcard will help attenuate the poor results of the increase in postal rates.

On the other hand, the current rate has not frightened those who resisted this projected innovation because they feared a gross reduction in our finances. We had to reconcile an overly prudent approach with the adoption of a measure that other reforms made indispensable.

France was in danger of being the only country in Europe, other than Turkey, to be without the postcard which has been adopted, or is in the process of being adopted everywhere else. Even with this high postal rate we could no longer deprive ourselves of this innovation. It was necessary to enter into an avenue that can only grow with time and would provide us with multiple advantages in many ways.

In England the postcard was introduced in 1870 at the rate of one half penny, or half the rate of an ordinary letter. The average number of missives without envelopes that are being mailed has

risen to one and a half million per week. For the year of 1871 more than seventy-five million went though the mail. It is expected that 1872 will see this number surpassed.

Far from diminishing the number of ordinary letters going through the mail, as was expected by many, their numbers have increased. In place of 863 million letters transported in 1870, the number has risen to 915 million in 1872. This enormous growth of fifty-two million letters has surpassed the average growth rate of the five previous years from 1866 to 1870. Previously the figure was 4%, now it is 6%.

Is there any clearer proof of the fiscal value of the postcard? Further on we will see how this is confirmed in other countries. As countries familiarize themselves with the postcard it finds more and more uses. Indeed, it is not only used in England as a means for families to transmit brief messages. The postcard is also used to send out invitations, to announce meetings, lectures, or gatherings of all sorts on the side of the card reserved for the message. In England we have seen postcards with commercial advertisements, or even with moral and religious instruction. Thoughts circulate everywhere now thanks to this inexpensive means of communication.

In Germany the carte-correspondence was decreed by the prince, then Count of Bismark, in June 1870 just before the outbreak of the war. This card entered into circulation on July 1, 1870 and was well received everywhere even though the postal rate was equal to the ordinary letter. It was only on July 1, 1872 that their rate was cut in half. This shows that the German government did not fall prey to fears of a reduction of postal revenue. In fact this fear was not justified as the number of ordinary letters in circulation has risen from 205 million in 1870 to 240 million in 1871.

A variation on the postcard, an improvement, in fact, has been put into operation in Holland, Belgium, Switzerland and other countries and recently in Germany. Along with the carte-correspondence is the *double* card. This is two cards, one to send, the other to be used for the answer, each with the stamp already affixed to the card. This most useful development will undoubtedly further increase the popularity of this ingenious mode of communication.

Nothing will make us appreciate the usefulness of the postcard than the following letter from an administrator known by all, Mr. Stephan, Postmaster General of the German Empire.

We reproduce it here in its entirety.

"The rate of the postcard introduced in Germany on July 1, 1870 has been reduced since July 1.

They are treated like letters and their stamping is obligatory. They can be sent by Express Mail as any ordinary piece of mail. The carte-correspondence found favor with the public quickly. Their numbers continue to increase. In Berlin alone, 8 to 10,000 cards circulate a day with no reduction in the number of ordinary letters. The postcard, while in some cases having replaced the ordinary letter, is to be considered as a new class of mail, distinct from other classes of mail. The number of exchanges effected, both commercial and familial, offers a great advantage as they can be used while on vacation, or to place an order with a merchant or a bookseller.

Cases of abuse carried out with this new means of communication, notably in England, have rarely occurred in Germany. This is similar to cases of a like nature carried out with the letter sent in an envelope when injurious things were written on the envelope itself to be seen by all in their course. Postal employees are invited to not deliver cards of this nature." Thus the resolution voted by the National Assembly on December 10th, 1872 has the advantage of including France in a system that all countries, with the exception of Turkey, will gain from. When all the world is marching, the country that does not advance goes backward. We have averted this unfortunate destiny.

—Louis Wolowski
Berlin, November 1872

Bibliography

Aronson, Rudolph. *Theatrical and Musical Memoirs.* New York: McBride, Nast & Co., 1913.

Austen, Jessica Tyler, ed. *Moses Coit Tyler, 1835–1900: Selections from his Letters and Diaries.* Garden City, NY: Doubleday, 1911.

Bassett, Fred. *"Wish You Were Here! The Story of the Golden Age of Picture Postcards in the United States."* Appendix C to The New York State Library Postcard Collection. Online Source. <http://www.nysl.nysed.gov/msscfa/qc16510ess.htm>.

Belford's Monthly Magazine. Toronto: Belford Brothers, Publishers, 1877–1878.

Belloc, Alexis. *Les Postes Francaises: Recherches Historiques sur leur Origine, leur Développement, leur Legislation.* Paris: Firmin-Didot, 1886.

Benjamin, S. G. W. "Ocean Steamships—1882—Crossing the Atlantic in the Late 1800's." Century Illustrated Monthly Magazine 24 (October 1882): 666–78. Rpt. at <www.gjenvick.com/SteamshipArticles/1882-OceanSteamships.html>.

Carline, Richard. *Pictures in the Post: The Story of the Picture Postcard.* Bedford: Gordon Fraser, 1959.

Charbon, Paul. *Quelle Belle Invention que la Poste!* Paris: Éditions Gallimard, 1991.

Cook, Joel. *A Holiday Tour in Europe.* Philadelphia: Lippincott, 1879. [c1878].

Corkett, Frederick T. "The Production and Collection of the Pictorial Postcard." Journal of the Society of Arts. 1906.

Dangcil, Tommy. *Hollywood 1900–1950 in Vintage Postcards.* Hollywood: Arcadia Publishing, 2002.

Economides, Stephen. "Heinrich von Stephan and the Unification of the German Postal System." Winton M. Blount Symposium on Postal History. Smithsonian National Postal Museum, Washington, D.C. November 4, 2006.

Fitch, George. "Upon the Threatened Extinction of the Art of Letter Writing." *American Magazine* 70 (June 1910): 172–5.

Guyonnet, Georges. *La Carte Postale Illustrée.* Paris: Chambre syndicale française de la carte postale illustrée, [c. 1947].

Harrington, John Walker. "Postal Carditis and Some Allied Manias." *American Magazine* 61 (March 1906): 562–7.

Kyrou, Ado. *L'âge d'Or de la Carte Postale.* Paris: A. Balland, 1975.

Macy, John Albert. *A Guide to Reading for Young and Old.* Garden City: Doubleday, 1913. c. 1910.

Miller, George and Dorothy. *Picture Postcards in the United States, 1893–1918.* New York: Crown, 1976.

Monahan, Valerie. *Collecting Postcards in Colour, 1914–1930.* Poole: Blandford Press, 1980.

Neudin, Joëlle. *L'Argus International des Cartes Postales de Collection.* Paris: Éditions Image-document, 1977–1980.

Newell, Martin L. *The Law of Slander and Libel in*

Civil and Criminal Cases. 1890. 3rd edition. Mason Harder Newell. Chicago: Callaghan, 1914.

O'Reilly, Patrick. *Bulletin de la Société Archéologique, Historique et Artistique.* Le Vieux Papier. Fascicule No. 238. November 1970.

Rogan, Bjarne. "An Entangled Object: The Picture Postcard as Souvenir and Collectible, Exchange and Ritual Communication." *Cultural Analysis* 4 (2005). <http://socrates.berkeley.edu/~caforum/>.

Rothschild, Arthur baron de. *Histoire de la Poste aux Lettres et du Timbre-poste Depuis leurs Origines Jusqu'à nos Jours.* Bruxelles, J.B. Moëns, 1876.

The Spatula: A Magazine for Pharmacists. Boston: Spatula Pub. Co., 1894–1935. June 1914

Staff, Frank. *The Picture Postcard & its Origins.* New York: Frederick Praeger, 1966.

United States Congress, Committee on Ways and Means. *Tariff Hearings Before the Committee on Ways and Means of the House of Representatives, Sixtieth Congress, 1908-1909.* Vol 8. Washington: GPO, 1909. 9 vols.

Willoughby, Martin. *A History of Postcards: A Pictorial Record from the Turn of the Century to the Present Day.* London: Studio Editions, 1992.

Wolowski, Louis. "The Post Card in Different Countries." *Journal des Économistes* (January to March, 1873): 90-96.

Zeyons, Serge. *Les Cartes Postales.* Paris: Hachette, 1979.